The Christian life was never meant to be defined by the information you knew *about* God—the information should summon us into relationship. Jesus defined eternal life as *knowing God*. This speaks of intimacy, encounter, and experience. This is the essence of Patricia Bootsma's new book, *A Lifestyle of Divine Encounters*. She is calling you to step beyond knowing information about God to actually knowing Him personally and powerfully.

Patricia doesn't write from the position of an ivory tower spectator, offering spiritual theory. She has lived and led in the midst of a global move of God for over 20 years, and her words come from her love of the scripture and her real-life experience. This book provides solid biblical teaching that refuses to let you live on the spiritual sidelines.

Get ready to see prayer and the Word of God in a whole new, experiential dimension. And depending on where you are in your knowledge of the prophetic and prophetic ministry, I know Patricia's teaching will be a blessing to you, as she is a Word-based prophetic voice who will teach how to access the prophetic language of the Holy Spirit.

I love the practical approach of this book. It is an easy read. So many want to know how to live a lifestyle where God encounters are normal, not the exception. This book doesn't provide some static formula; however, it does offer a time-tested road map that many have traveled and experienced results from—prayer, prophecy, and the living Word of God. Patricia is the real deal and she has a godly marriage and large family of children in their early adult years who are following the Lord. This alone makes her worth listening to.

—MIKE BICKLE
International House of Prayer, Kansas City
Best-selling author of *Growing in Prayer* and
Growing in the Prophetic

Patricia Bootsma is a humble yet powerful woman. She carries God's love and kindness and walks in close communion with Him. She lives what she so eloquently teaches. This book is full of wisdom and practical guidance birthed in the place of prayer and relationship with God as well as historical examples. Read this and grow in hunger for connection with God through prayer, prophecy, and His word!

—HEIDI G. BAKER, PhD
Co-Founder and CEO of Iris Global

I deeply honor and respect Patricia Bootsma. She loves the Spirit and the Word. She is both pastoral and prophetic and is a magnificent, humble, and authentic leader who is willing to share profound, yet practical revelation and impartation she has gleaned over her many years of walking closely with God. Her book, *A Lifestyle of Divine Encounters* will surely empower and equip you.

—DR. PATRICIA KING
www.patriciakingmentor.com

Few people have authority to speak on "Equipping All Believers" like Patricia Bootsma. She has spent her life equipping her six children, then equipping the churches that she and her husband have pastored, and finally equipping people to do the First Commandment in the houses of prayer she has built. Patricia Bootsma speaks with great authority on this key biblical truth—that all believers are called to extend the Kingdom of God...all for the glory of its King.

—Stacey Campbell
wesleystaceycampbell.com
Author of *Ecstatic Prophecy*

Early last fall, I shared with our church that I was in pursuit of divine encounters. Each ministry trip was a fulfillment of that desire. In London, my dear friends, Stu and Chloe Glassborow kept telling me about this "amazing woman" named Patricia Bootsma and that I just had to meet her. In less than a month, she was praying for my wife, Barbara and me — a divine encounter! Patricia's new book will whet the appetite of anyone desiring to go beyond the shallows into the deeps of the Holy Spirit. It is biblically sound and is itself a Divine Encounter.

—Bishop Joseph L. Garlington, Sr.
Presiding Bishop
Reconciliation! an International Network
of Churches and Ministries
Author of *Worship*

Patricia Bootsma's prayer is grounded in prophetic gift. When someone prophesies who also prays, it is like having insurance for your words! You know that the continued soaking of a person will naturally influence the words and tone of what is communicated. The words will carry the heart of the Father. Patricia is a treasure for the church. This book sums up this powerful marriage of prayer and the prophetic. I recommend it highly to those who want to know how to lean heavy into greater purity in the prophetic.

—Steve Witt
Pastor, Bethel Cleveland
Author of *Voices*

Seldom does a short book provide both depth and breadth on the topic it covers. Patricia Bootsma's book *A Lifestyle of Divine Encounters* achieves that sought-after goal. Brimming with fresh revelation, Patricia makes alive and penetrating many of the foundational stones of our Christian lives: prayer, Bible study, hearing God's voice, and prophetic evangelism. The book is worth it just for the chapter including Godly declarations. Don't read this book unless you are willing to get out of your comfort zone, reorganize yourself, and let your God-life get deeper and bolder. Inspiration awaits you if you say yes.

—CHESTER AND BETSY KYLSTRA
Founders, Restoring the Foundations Ministry

A LIFESTYLE OF
DIVINE
Encounters

THROUGH PRAYER, PROPHECY, AND THE LIVING WORD

PATRICIA BOOTSMA

DESTINY IMAGE® PUBLISHERS, INC.

P.O. Box 310, Shippensburg, PA 17257-0310

"Promoting Inspired Lives."

This book and all other Destiny Image and Destiny Image Fiction books are available at Christian bookstores and distributors worldwide.

Cover design by Eileen Rockwell
Interior design by Terry Clifton

For more information on foreign distributors, call 717-532-3040.

Reach us on the Internet: www.destinyimage.com.

ISBN 13 TP: 978-0-7684-1882-8
ISBN 13 eBook: 978-0-7684-1883-5
ISBN 13 HC: 978-0-7684-1885-9
ISBN 13 LP: 978-0-7684-1884-2

For Worldwide Distribution, Printed in the U.S.A.

2 3 4 5 6 7 8 / 22 21 20 19 18

DEDICATION

This book is first of all dedicated to the fathers and mothers who have helped shape me into who I am today.

To Siebren Hart and Jean Boersma—my parents. Thanks for raising me to love God, love His Word and make sure I'm in church!

To John and Carol Arnott—my spiritual parents. You have taught me so much about getting my heart healed, knowing my Heavenly Father's love, and how to live a life flowing with the Spirit. I'll be forever grateful to the Lord for having you in my life.

To Mike Bickle—a friend and mentor. Thank you for pressing into prayer and the Word as you have. I am a life impacted by your ministry. And thanks for hiring my daughter!

This book is also dedicated to my family:

To John, my amazing husband. I love so many things about you and especially your heart after God.

To our children: Judah married to Bethany and grandkids Josiah, Hasten and Fairlight; Gabrielle married to Benji Nunez; Aquila married to Yannick Tendon; and Phoebe, Zoe and Glory Anna.

I'm so glad I'm your mother. You are all a delight to my heart. Let's keep pressing into Jesus together. He is worth it all!

This book is also dedicated to the reader. My prayer for you is the power of the Holy Spirit would come upon you as you read these words, that you would be compelled to live a life of divine encounters, never be the same again, and run the race for the prize of Jesus Christ.

Lastly, I want to dedicate this work to You, Lord. Thank you for loving me as You do. May my life be ever lived to know You and make You known.

CONTENTS

FOREWORD

A Lifestyle of Divine Encounters is a must-read for every person who desires to be closer to God, and to live out their life's mission in power and great fruitfulness. Seriously, it is really, really good! In one way, the title says it all!

I have known Patricia ever since she was a teenager who turned up at the first church that Carol and I planted back in 1981 in Stratford, Ontario, Canada. Jubilee Christian Fellowship was soon replete with young people and she became one of the most eager, joining in during the mid to late '80s. She had a great hunger for the Word of God and a great desire to deal with the hurts and fears in her own life, to be all the better positioned to walk in the Anointing before the Lord with clean hands and a pure heart. She wanted to help people through fruitful ministry.

I remember when she left for the University of London in London, Ontario, to study nursing, which she handily completed, graduating and becoming a registered nurse; while there she facilitated a home group of other youth who learned about and encountered the Lord under her influence and leadership. Her career took her to Toronto, where right at the time we were beginning our Toronto church as a small group in my mother's living room. Not infrequently, Patricia would be there as well, worshipping, receiving, and contributing.

Throughout these years, Carol and Patricia became very close and spent many hours together, working through the issues of the heart for healing, cleansing, and freedom. She was at the forefront of us developing our core values of FIRE:. Receiving a revelation of the Father's love; Intimacy and learning to hear His voice; Restoration, healing and sanctification through repentance and forgiveness for hurts, wounds, shame, pain, anger, and fear; and finally; Equipping believers for ministry and evangelism, by the gifts of the Spirit through the fruits and power of the Spirit.

As I began reading the galleys of *A Lifestyle of Divine Encounters*, I instantly realized that Patricia has an amazing grasp of the aforementioned FIRE values, and in addition, has blended all that with an intimate and powerful prayer life that enables and empowers her to have a full working knowledge of these values, and to be the mighty woman of God and amazing wife and mother that she is.

I am very pleased and excited to recommend *A Lifestyle of Divine Encounters* to you. It is a powerful how-to, step-by-step manual for you to enter into, and not only maintain, but grow in the necessary steps and stages of a revival lifestyle. She will teach you to pray, and not just pray, but pray with joy and fervent effectiveness, which is so lacking in the body of Christ today. When John and Patricia returned to our Toronto church, after a season away leading our Stratford church, one of her first missions was to ramp up our House of Prayer to include the youth of our School of Ministry and many others, bringing Harp and Bowl ministry—Worship and Prayer together. It resurrected the Tabernacle of David ministry among us for many hours every day. Also, you will discover her amazing grasp of, and love for the Word of God, as it is the basis and final authority of all that we teach and do.

I particularly enjoyed Patricia's teaching on prophetic ministry. It would be fair to say that this is one of her strong suits, right along with prayer. She explains and teaches prophetic ministry so well and in such a balanced way, that it would set any pastor's heart at ease to have this kind of cutting-edge teaching brought with such helpful checks and balances included and taught to their prophetic and intercessory people. *(that group is sometimes the pastor's nightmare :-))*.

If you take a look at the various chapter titles in the opening pages, you will note that this is a book centered around Prayer, Prophecy and the Word of God. But don't be fooled by a superficial or casual glance. *A Lifestyle of Divine Encounters* is a serious instructional manual for those who want to press into a deep and meaningful relationship with our wonderful trinitarian God. I was so impressed with the maturity and experience that accompanied these teachings, and I found them all so very helpful and practical, that Carol and I plan to go through this entire book again, slowly and meditatively, applying each and every chapter of this book to our hearts for our own growth and devotions. I find it so exciting that we can now learn such deep, meaningful and functional truth from one of our spiritual daughters, of whom we are very proud.

This is a very practical piece for us all. You will not be confused or bewildered by what Patricia brings. Again and again, you will find yourself agreeing that this need in your life that is being uncovered is important, and yet it is not out of reach for you. With the practical steps that are being offered, you will clearly see that this needs to become a value and goal for your life. If you are even considering this book, then it is because you are hungering and thirsting for the realities of God to become even more powerful and effective your life. Personally, I found this to be an absolutely amazing book. I was surprised by how good it is. (Though knowing Patricia, I shouldn't have been.) It truly is a manual that will take established, yet hungry Christians onward and upward to a whole new fruitful life experience in the God of love and power. The truths and revealed insights are bathed in prayer, fueled by revelation yet seasoned and tested with the rigors of over 20 years of pastoral and itinerant ministry. It IS going to bless you richly!

Well done, Patricia, for a very practical, helpful and needed resource for those of us in the Body of Christ today who are contending for a fuller life in the Spirit as we pray and believe for the greatest outpouring of the Holy Spirit since the book of Acts, and the greatest harvest of souls ever to flood the halls of Heaven, and all before the soon return of our wonderful Savior and Lord, Messiah Jesus.

—JOHN ARNOTT
Founding Pastor,
Catch the Fire, Toronto

INTRODUCTION

We are given one life to live on this earth, one shot to give ourselves to what really counts—or to waste the breath of life given to us. Our time in the flesh on planet earth is so very short, perhaps 80, 90, or slightly more years, compared to forever in eternity. There is a question that must be asked of every one of humankind's members, "What is the purpose of life?"

Thankfully, the very One who spoke our life into existence has given us the answer. Known as the Great Commandment, Jesus said, "*You shall love the Lord your God with all your heart, with all your soul, and with all your mind.' This is the first and great commandment. And the second is like it: 'You shall love your neighbor as yourself.' On these two commandments hang all the Law and the Prophets*" (Matt. 22:37-40).

If loving God is the greatest goal, along with loving others and ourselves, another question arises: "How can we give ourselves to this purpose?"

This book is about pressing into the heart of God through prayer, prophecy, and the study of His Word. May it be used of the Holy Spirit to challenge every reader to give themselves to what really counts in the light of eternity and make needed adjustments to align with the will of the Father in Heaven.

The Apostle Paul learned much about the importance of life, having first been a murderous zealot. Having an encounter with the living Christ, he then gave the rest of his life for the cause of spreading truth. He speaks these words:

> *But what things were gain to me, these I have counted loss for Christ. Yet indeed I also count all things loss for the excellence of the knowledge of Christ Jesus my Lord, for whom I have suffered the loss of all things, and count them as rubbish, that I may gain Christ and be found in Him, not having my own righteousness, which is from that law, but that which is through faith in Christ, the righteousness which is from God by faith; that I may know Him and the power of His resurrection, and the fellowship of His sufferings, being conformed to His death, if, by any means, I may attain to the resurrection from the dead. Not that I have already attained, or am already perfected; but I press on, that I may lay hold of that for which Christ Jesus has also laid hold of me. Brethren, I do not count myself to have apprehended; but one thing I do, forgetting those things which are behind and reaching forward to those things which are ahead, I press toward the goal for the prize of the upward call of God in Christ Jesus* (Philippians 3:7-14).

There is a goal above any goal in life. There is a prize higher than any prize. It is this: to know and love the One who gave us the very breath that sustains our life. He is worthy of pressing in for, of giving ourselves to wholeheartedly. We will never regret having made Jesus Christ and the pursuit of His heart our number-one aim. We will only be abundantly blessed, not only in this life but also in the life to come.

Our culture will tell us to chase the American dream, or that we can only be "somebody" if we are beautiful, smart, rich, or powerful. The Word of God counters the lies: *"Thus says the Lord: 'Let not the wise man glory in his wisdom, let not the mighty man glory in his might, nor let the rich man glory in his riches; but let him who glories glory in this, that he understands and knows Me, that I am the Lord, exercising lovingkindness, judgment and righteousness in the earth. For in these I delight,' says the Lord"* (Jer. 9:23-24). Growing in knowing, growing in loving, that is what counts in life. We can embrace a countercultural and fully biblical definition of success: "I am loved by God, I love God, therefore I am a success."

As we pray, our hearts become awakened in communion with Him. As we seek to live a prophetic life our hearts leap up when He speaks to us (see Song of Sol. 5:6). As we seek to study the Word of God, we come to the Living Word through the written Word.

This book is about cultivating dynamic devotion and whole-hearted, focused pursuit of Jesus Christ. It is about growth into the mature Bride of Christ, ready for a celestial wedding to come.

As I study the Word and church history, I see a common thread among the leaders the Lord has particularly used to make a great impact on the earth. They are the ones with an abandoned passionate love for Him, a diligence to obey the call on their lives, and fearlessness in facing adversity and opposition.

They are burning and shining lamps. They stand out from the culture around them. They are ones who carry the glory, make a difference, and pay the price. The famous quote rings in my ears, "Catch on fire and others will love to come watch you burn."

Madame Guyon, a French contemplative from the 17th century, spoke of living in abandonment. "It is a matter of being enveloped by God and possessed by Him. Abandonment is a matter of the greatest importance if you are going to make progress in knowing your Lord. Abandonment is, in fact, the key to the inner court—the key to the fathomless depths. Abandonment is the key to the inward spiritual life."[1]

First Corinthians 6:17 says, *"But he who is joined to the Lord is one spirit with Him."* Oneness with the Lord has everything to do with His Spirit inhabiting our being. Our hands become His hands; our heart, His heart; our mouth, His mouth. To be completely surrendered and submitted and continually filled with His Spirit, there is need for cultivating union with Him, an abiding in His Presence.

Jesus used a beautiful analogy: *"I am the vine, you are the branches. He who abides in Me, and I in him, bears much fruit; for without Me you can do nothing"* (John 15:5). As we abide, we bear fruit. It is fruit that looks like us being transformed more and more into His image. We gain strong character, moral excellence, joy, peace, anointing, and become fruitful in every area of our lives.

In this book, we will examine abiding with the Lord in prayer, in His voice, and in His Word. My prayer is that all who read these pages would be forever changed, continually pressing into the heart of the Father with abandonment and passion.

May we echo the words of King David, the man after God's own heart: *"One thing I have desired of the Lord, that will I seek: That I may dwell in the house of the Lord all the days of my life, to behold the beauty of the Lord, and to inquire in His temple"* (Ps. 27:4).

Prayer

Chapter 1

WHY PRAY?

Lord, teach us to pray.
—LUKE 11:1

*T*he 12 had walked with the Master for some time. They had seen demons cast out, wind and waves stilled, food multiplied, the sick healed, the dead raised. They themselves had been given authority and power over all demons and to cure diseases (see Luke 9:1). They had gone out to preach the Kingdom of God, healing the sick along the way. The 70 had similarly been sent out preaching, healing, and with joy demonstrating the Kingdom. The power encounters were so spectacular satan was seen falling like lightning from Heaven (see Luke 10:18).

After all that, the passage of Luke 11:1 is recorded: *"Now it came to pass, as He was praying in a certain place, when He ceased, that one of His disciples said to Him, 'Lord, teach us to pray, as John also taught his disciples.'"*

The disciples realized something was missing in their personal walk with God, and it had to do with observing their leader's prayer life. Jesus, the Son of God, who had stepped out of Heaven for His assignment on earth, knew He needed to stay in communion with the Father in prayer. He modeled getting away from the busyness of life, even scaling a mountain to get alone. Theologians estimate Jesus spent four to six hours a day in prayer.

If the incarnate Christ needed to pray, so do we. If the disciples who walked with Jesus in the flesh and performed great miracles in His name needed to learn to pray, so do we. In the words of Bill Johnson, founder of Bethel Church in Redding, California, "Communication with the Spirit was the secret to Christ's ministry, and it is the secret to ours."[2]

If we are to echo the disciples cry—"Lord, teach us to pray"— let us first examine why we would want to develop a mature prayer life in the Lord.

RELATIONSHIP

The greatest aim in prayer must center on the communion we have with a personal God who longs for relationship with us. Just as any relationship is enhanced by communication, so it is with mortal man and the majestic God.

Billy Graham said it well, "Prayer is a two-way conversation with God." As we will explore later, God isn't expecting us to do all of the talking!

Relationship with the Lord is enhanced by a regular, diligent prayer life. The positioning of ourselves before God in prayer places us close to the fire of His love for us. Drawing near to Him, He draws near to us (James 4:8).

Priests

I was awakened one morning at 2:30 A.M. and prompted by the Lord to read in Ezekiel, starting in chapter 40. I sleepily read through chapter after chapter about the temple Ezekiel describes, but I was suddenly alert and felt revelation come as I read Ezekiel 44. This chapter speaks of the priests and their duty before the Lord, and uses the words "shame" and "abominations" to describe the priests who neglected their position before the Lord. Four tasks are used to illustrate the inner court role of the priests: *"But the priests…shall come near Me to minister to Me; and they shall stand before Me…and they shall keep My charge"* (Ezek. 44:15-16). The priests were called to come near, minister to the Lord, stand before Him, and keep His charge. This was done in the inner court wearing their linen garments. Later they could take off their priestly garments to go into the outer court to minister to the people. Ezekiel 44:28 further clarifies the special position of the priest, *"It shall be, in regard to their inheritance, that I am their inheritance. You shall give them no possession in Israel, for I am their possession."*

When Jesus came and died, the curtain of the temple was torn in two, from top to bottom. God tore it! There was great significance to this act. The shed blood of Jesus ushered in a new era where priests were no longer required to offer animal sacrifices as atonement for sin.

Who are the priests of today? We are! Revelation 1:6 says, *"And (Jesus) has made us kings and priests to His God and Father."* First Peter 2:9 says, *"But you are a chosen generation, a royal priesthood, a holy nation, His own special people, that you may proclaim the praises of Him who called you out of darkness into His marvelous light."*

Our "duty," or really *privilege*, is to "come near, minister to the Lord, stand before Him and keep His charge." After we have prioritized that priestly duty, then we can be the kings He has called us to be, operating in the dominion mandate of Genesis 1 to rule in our sphere of influence. We can minister to the people in the outer court with effectiveness once we have ministered to the Lord in the inner court.

Ministry to God

How do we minister to the God who created the universe? How could mere man affect the One who sustains their very life?

God said at Creation, *"Let Us make man in Our image, according to Our likeness; let them have dominion over the fish of the sea, over the birds of the air, and over the cattle, over all the earth and over every creeping thing that creeps on the earth.' So God created man in His own image; in the image of God He created him; male and female He created them"* (Gen. 1:26-27). Unlike the creatures created prior to this moment, man received the special call of being created in God's image to rule and reign on the earth through close relationship with the Creator.

Later, coming to relate to the ones made in His image, the Father called, "Where are you?" Adam and Eve were hiding from the Presence of the Lord. In their case, they were hiding because of the shame of disobedience. Today, many of those made in God's image are still hiding from Him. It may be due to busyness, lack of interest, unbelief, other priorities, or a dullness of heart. This hiding, or removing ourselves from drawing near, standing before, ministering to and keeping the charge of the Lord, equates to neglecting our priestly duties before Him. In the words of Ezekiel, this would be an abomination. Stating it another way, it is a tragedy.

Henri Nouwen in his book *In the Name of Jesus* states, "The original meaning of the word, 'theology' was union with God in prayer. Today, theology has become one academic discipline alongside many others and often theologians are finding it hard to pray."[3]

DIRECTION

Our Father in Heaven created us for greatness. Ephesians 2:10 states, *"For we are His workmanship, created in Christ Jesus for good works, which God prepared beforehand that we should walk in them."* Since it is God who created us for these great works, it is God who also helps reveal to us what His particular plan is for each of us.

Clarity from the Spirit

> But as it is written, 'Eye has not seen, nor ear heard, nor have entered into the heart of man the things which God has prepared for those who love Him.' But God has revealed them to us through His Spirit. For the Spirit searches all things, yes, the deep things of God. For what man knows the things of a man except the spirit of the man which is in him? Even so no one knows the things of God except the Spirit of God. Now we have received, not the spirit of the world, but the Spirit who is from God, that we might know the things that have been freely given to us by God (1 Corinthians 2:9-12).

As this passage makes clear, the Spirit of God within us helps us know what the Father has for us. Our part of this equation is to ask for that wisdom, direction, and clarity of His leadership for our lives. As we ask, He answers. Doors open or close, clarity comes into our spirit, a path is highlighted before us.

A few years ago, we were praying for clarity for the future of our daughter Gabrielle as she was finishing her high school studies. We discussed different possibilities, prayed together, and implored the Lord for His leadership. Months later, in a divine connection, the doors swung wide for Gabrielle to attend the International House of Prayer University in Kansas City. After her graduation, the ministry of International House of Prayer hired her and she now lives and works alongside her husband also on staff at IHOP-KC. Our prayers for direction certainly proved effective, even as they have multitudes of other times.

Wisdom

James 1:5 states, *"If any of you lacks wisdom, let him ask of God, who gives to all liberally and without reproach, and it will be given to him."* Wisdom in the Greek is *sophia*, meaning "practical wisdom, prudence, skill, insight, or right application of knowledge needed for guidance and direction." Surely we all need God's direction in the many decisions we make in life. All we need to do is ask, as God admonishes us in Jeremiah 33:3: *"Call to Me, and I will answer you, and show you great and mighty things, which you do not know."*

FRUITFULNESS

Jesus taught what was necessary to be fruitful. He stated, *"I am the vine, you are the branches. He who abides in Me, and I in him, bears much fruit; for without Me you can do nothing…You did not choose Me, but I chose you and appointed you that you should go and bear fruit, and that your fruit should remain, that whatever you ask the Father in My name He may give you"* (John 15:5,16). Just as a branch hoping to yield fruit can produce nothing if not connected to the vine, similarly, we are barren of harvest if detached from the Giver of life.

If we want to be fruitful in all things, the main activity to pursue is abiding in Christ. We can abide with Him in His Presence, in His Word, in His voice, and with Him in prayer. Mike Bickle, founder and leader of the International House of Prayer in Kansas

City said, "He has much to say, but He allows us to set the pace of the conversation with Him. If we start the conversation, He will continue it as long as we do. When we stop it, He stops it and waits until we begin again. Abiding in Christ involves an ongoing conversation that consists of many 10 to 20 second exchanges, strengthened by longer prayer times."[4]

POWER/DIVINE ASSISTANCE

The connection in prayer to the heart and power of the God who holds the universe in the palm of His hand gives us access to ultimate power. Do you need breakthrough in your job, relationships, marriage, finances, health, and creativity? Ask of God. James 5:16 states, *"The effective, fervent prayer of a righteous man avails much."*

Lou Engle, leader of The Call, states, "History belongs to the intercessor."[5] Dick Eastman, director of Every Home for Christ, adds, "Praying Christians are society's best revolutionaries."[6] There are many stories from history that validate such views.

Charles Finney

Charles Finney stirred revival fires across America's eastern states in the first half of the 19th century. It has been recorded that 2.5 million people came to salvation through his preaching. There was an instrumental member of Finney's team named Father Nash who would travel weeks ahead to cities Finney was going to hold a crusade. Father Nash would pray for those cities and for the power of God to come in the crusade meetings.

One eyewitness recounts, "Charles Finney so realized the need of God's working in all his service that he was wont to send godly Father Nash on in advance to pray down the power of God into the meetings which he was about to hold." Not only did Nash prepare the communities for preaching, but he also continued in prayer during the meetings. "Often Nash would not attend meetings, and while Finney was preaching Nash was praying for the Spirit's outpouring upon him. Finney stated, 'I did the preaching altogether, and brother Nash gave himself up almost continually to prayer.' Often while the evangelist preached to the multitudes, Nash in some adjoining house would be upon his face in an agony of prayer, and God answered in the marvels of His grace. With all due credit to Mr. Finney for what was done, it was the praying men who held the ropes. The tears they shed, the groans they uttered are written in the book of the chronicles of the things of God."[7]

Reinhard Bonnke

Reinhard Bonnke, known as the most effective evangelist with nearly 75 million registered decisions for Christ, knows the power of prayer. For many years Suzette Hattingh was his main intercessor, sometimes praying under the very stage from which Reinhard was preaching.[8]

Rees Howells

Rees Howells was a dedicated man of prayer establishing orphanages and Bible schools. Rees was powerfully used of the Lord in prayer in World War II. Rees was involved in what is known as the miracle of Salerno. Allied troops in Salerno, Italy in 1943 prepared to march to Rome. The following is an eyewitness account:

> We had the first evening prayer meeting as usual in the conference hall, and gathered again at 9:45 P.M. The meeting had a solemn tone from the outset. "The Director, Mr. Howells, voice trembling with the burden of his message and scarcely audible, said, 'The Lord has burdened me between the meetings with the

invasion at Salerno. I believe our men are in great danger of losing their hold."

Howells then called the congregation of Bible students to prayer. It was not an ordinary prayer time. Prayer was intense and urgent, and in the greatest sense, true prevailing prayer. Howells relates, "The Spirit took hold of us and suddenly broke right through in the prayers, and we found ourselves praising and rejoicing, believing that God had heard and answered. We could not go on praying any longer so we rose... the Spirit witnessing in all our hearts that God had wrought some miraculous intervention in Italy. The victory was so outstanding that I looked at the clock as we rose to sing. It was the stroke of 11:00 P.M."

The story continues with amazing tribute to the value of persistent prayer. Several days later one of the local newspapers displayed the headline in large print, "The Miracle of Salerno." A front line reporter gave his personal account of the battle. He was with the advanced troops in the Salerno invasion on Monday. The enemy was advancing rapidly, and increasing devastation was evident. It was obvious that unless a miracle happened the city would be lost. British troops had insufficient strength to stop the advance until the beachhead was established. Suddenly, with no reason, firing ceased and deathlike stillness settled. The reporter describes the next few moments, "We waited in breathless anticipation but nothing happened. I looked at my watch—it was eleven o'clock at night. Still we waited but still nothing happened; and nothing happened all night, but those hours made all the difference to the invasion. By morning the beachhead was established."[9]

OBEDIENCE

Another reason to pray is because God instructs us to do so. In the Sermon on the Mount, Jesus admonishes the believers to *"Ask, and it will be given to you; seek, and you will find; knock, and it will be opened to you"* (Matt. 7:7). He also three times states, *"When you pray…"* (Matt. 6:5,6,7). A vibrant prayer life of followers of Jesus was expected as part of the their call.

In relation to noticing the multitudes weary, scattered and without a shepherd, Jesus, moved with compassion, said to His disciples, *"The harvest truly is plentiful, but the laborers are few. Therefore pray the Lord of the harvest to send out laborers into His harvest"* (Matt. 9:37-38). We have experienced firsthand the greater effectiveness in soul winning if first prayer is raised. Habits of prayer build habits of evangelism. Habits of evangelism build God's Kingdom.

Many years ago, several young Salvation Army officers asked founding leader General Booth, "How can we win souls?" Booth's return wire communication stated only two words: "Try tears."[10] He knew the effectiveness of travailing prayer in obedience to Jesus' admonition to make disciples and firstly begin with prayer.

Chapter 2

HOW TO PRAY

Charles Spurgeon declared, "Prayer in itself is an art which only the Holy Ghost can teach us. He is the giver of all prayer. Pray for prayer—pray until you can pray." [11] Dick Eastman said, "To learn prayer we must pray. We only learn prayer's deepest depths in prayer, not from books. We reach prayer's highest heights in prayer, not from sermons. The only place to learn prayer is in prayer, bent and broken on our knees. Prayer is a skill developed through experience. Learning to pray is like learning a trade. We are apprentices and must serve time at it."

Just as these great men of God articulate, prayer is learned by doing it. The Holy Spirit is a good teacher and He helps us in our weakness know how to grow in prayer. Even so, we will examine some practical tips on prayer.

TIPS ON PRAYER

Time

If you schedule time in your day for prayer and build a habit of prayer, it much more likely you will actually do it. Corrie ten

Boom, the Dutch survivor of Ravensbruck concentration camp, said, "Make an appointment with the King and keep your appointment with the King."[12] Perhaps it means waking earlier, taking time out of entertainment, or rearranging your schedule and saying no to other pressing demands to prioritize time in God's Presence.

There are numerous scriptural references to giving early morning hours to prayer. Jesus would rise before dawn or even pray all night (see Mark 1:35). David uttered, *"O God, You are my God; early will I seek You"* (Ps. 63:1), and Daniel had set prayer times three times a day (see Dan. 6:10). I recommend, if at all possible, to give the Lord morning hours while you are alert and fresh in strength. Giving God the leftovers after a busy, draining day may lead to falling asleep rather than spending quality time with the One most important to us.

Even with a set, special time to give ourselves to seeking the Lord in prayer, we can also continue in a spirit of prayer all through the day. First Thessalonians 5:16-18 says, *"Rejoice always, pray without ceasing, in everything give thanks; for this is the will of God in Christ Jesus for you."*

Remaining in an attitude of quiet prayer or communion with God throughout the day keeps the constant connection of two-way communication with the One who never slumbers or sleeps nor is ever too busy for us. Brother Lawrence wrote, "There is not in the world a kind of life more sweet and delightful than that of continual conversation with God. Those only can comprehend it who practice and experience it."[13]

Place

Having a quiet, comfortable, usual place to pray enhances our times of prayer. Some may have a favorite chair in the living room, others in their beds, or some may be fortunate enough to have a special room dedicated to prayer. I know of a Norwegian couple that actually added an upper level to their home to be designated as a scenic prayer room. Others have emptied out closets to be used as prayer rooms, such as skillfully portrayed in the hit movie "War Room."

We will discuss corporate prayer in a later section, but regarding personal prayer, Jesus admonished praying in "secret" (see Matt. 6:5-6). We are not to pray only in public to be seen by others so we can be portrayed as "spiritual." A prayer of thanks for the food we are about to eat at the dinner table is good. Yet if that or a nightly rendition of, "Now I lay me down to sleep…" is the extent of our prayer lives, there is a large gap in what is available for us in a life of prayer.

Praying with the TV on, the radio blaring, or other distractions around us can take away from hearing the whisper of the Holy Spirit in our hearts.

In Faith

James 1:6 says, *"But let him ask in faith, with no doubting, for he who doubts is like a wave of the sea driven and tossed by the wind."* Coming to the Lord in prayer, it is helpful to know that He actually hears us, is moved by our prayers, and we are accomplishing something. Paul said, *"Thus I fight: not as one who beats the air"* (1 Cor. 9:26) He knew the spiritual disciplines he engaged in accomplished much.

The Hebrews 11 "hall of fame" can also be called the "hall of faith," as the stories of heroes such as Enoch, Noah, Abraham, Moses, David, Samuel, and more tell of those who exemplified faith, defined as *"the substance of things hoped for, the evidence of things not seen"* (Heb. 11:1). We pray to a physically unseen God, obtaining the tangible through faith.

Persistence

Luke 18 gives the parable of the persistent widow. Her tenacity before an unjust judge led to her getting her request. Jesus equated her constancy with faith showing that similarly God will hear and answer the cry of His elect who persistently come before Him in prayer.

In this age of instant satisfaction, it is tempting to think God is like McDonalds: instant. Sometimes an answer may be delayed due to wrong motives, wrong timing, or an adjustment the Lord wants to make in our hearts that changes the prayer to align with His will. Proverbs 12:27 says, *"Diligence is man's precious possession."* That certainly applies to a diligence in prayer. John and I have prayed daily since our children were born for their future spouses. Three of our six children are married to exceptional, godly, amazing people and the last three are still too young to marry. How grateful we are for answered prayer, and how worth it to pray for such an important part of our children's destiny.

WAYS TO PRAY

There can be various ways or aspects to prayer. People will develop their own personal prayer history in God. Here are aspects of prayer I have found helpful.

Soaking

The term soaking may be better known as tarrying, or waiting on the Lord. Waiting on the Lord means drawing near to Him to simply "be" before we do anything, even "doing" prayer. Soaking can take on different forms for different people. It may be by playing your instrument and getting caught up in the Presence of the Lord, or sitting by the window looking at the birds in the backyard feeling the peace of God. It could mean abiding in the Presence of the Lord while meditating on the Word of God or by simply being still. Personally, I put the ear buds of an iPod in my ears and play anointed Christian instrumental music, and lay down resting in His Presence. I usually do this first thing when I awaken before I get out of bed, for anywhere between 10-60 minutes. I have been doing this for 15 years and it has radically changed my life.

I used to be a registered nurse, during which time I worked with intravenous drips giving needed liquids or medicine to needy patients. By analogy, when I soak, I feel as though I'm hooked up to a divine IV drip. I am strengthened in my soul, mind, and spirit with the fruit of the Spirit: love, joy, peace, patience, kindness, goodness, gentleness, faithfulness, and self-control. Practicing abiding in the Presence of the Lord has caused me to be a more loving person, more patient, more kind, and more sensitive to the voice of the Spirit.

Isaiah 40:31 states, *"But those who wait on the Lord shall renew their strength; they shall mount up with wings like eagles, they shall run and not be weary, they shall walk and not faint."* We cannot give what we do not receive. Soaking has to do with coming close to the heart of God and simply receiving. Subsequently, we are energized by the Spirit to live life out of a restful state full of God's Presence.

Worship

Jesus gave a prayer as a guide, known as the Lord's Prayer:

Our Father in Heaven, hallowed be Your name. Your kingdom come. Your will be done on earth as it is in heaven. Give us this day our daily bread. And forgive us our debts, as we forgive our debtors. And do not lead us into temptation, but deliver us from the evil one. For Yours is the kingdom and the power and the glory forever. Amen (Matthew 6:9-13).

The structure of this prayer has the components of worship, intercession, and worship. Defining worship as "agreement with who God is," the words *"Our Father in Heaven, hallowed be Your name"* convey reverence, as does *"For Yours is the kingdom and the power and the glory forever."* Worship is a part of prayer, even if it simply is stating the obvious: "You are God, I am not. I worship You."

Of course worship can also be when we raise our voice in song, join in musical symposiums of adoration, or bow the knee or prostrate ourselves in homage to the King. He is worthy of our worship.

Thanksgiving

Thanksgiving helps usher us not only into positive thoughts and emotions but helps us access the heart of God. *"Enter into His gates with thanksgiving, and into His courts with praise. Be thankful to Him, and bless His name"* (Ps. 100:4). Jonathan Edwards, the great revivalist, claimed that the affection of gratitude is one of the most accurate ways of finding the Presence of God in a person's life.

Thanksgiving is also to be a part of our supplications, our requests, before Him: *"Be anxious for nothing, but in everything by prayer and supplication, with thanksgiving, let your requests be made known to God"* (Phil. 4:6). As children, we of course ask our Father for what we need; isn't it good to thank Him for what He's already done for us? It blesses me when my children are grateful for what their dad and I do for them or give to them. Similarly, it must bless the Lord when we do not simply demand or take for granted all of His bountiful provisions for us, but come to Him with a heart of gratitude.

Around the table before meals, prayers of thanksgiving can be alternated between family members. We also like to hold hands as a family when we pray before a meal. We even do this in restaurants! It feels like we are connected as a family, connecting to a very real God to whom we are grateful for all He has done in giving us daily provision. Prayers of thanksgiving around the table are an excellent way for young children to learn an attitude of thanksgiving.

If one doesn't think they have much to be grateful for, digging a little deeper would reveal myriads of things to be thankful for: the breath of life, the ability to walk, see, talk or hear, family members, food to eat, the sun and rain, a place to live, clothes to wear, clean water, and not least of all, the shed blood of Jesus which paid the debt we owed. There are always things we can be thankful for if we would simply make the effort to identify them. Sometimes writing out a list of things one has to be thankful for can open understanding to all the good in life.

Listening/Journaling

Prayer is to be a two-way dialogue including receiving revelation from the Word of God and the words of God. Hearing the Lord through the still, small voice and receiving revelation from Him can be an important part of our prayer time. Prophetic intercession is a term to describe hearing the Lord for what specifically to pray. However, more on this will come in the section on prophecy.

CONFESSION

Since God knows all of our frailties anyway, it is good to be vulnerable, honest, and humble in our approach to God in prayer. Confession to Him of wayward thoughts, sin attitudes or whatever may be a gulf between oneself and a holy God are best confessed and repented of before Him. David even asked God to search him for those things he may not know about: *"Search me, O God, and know my heart; try me, and know my anxieties; and see if there is any wicked way in me, and lead me in the way everlasting"* (Ps. 139:23-24).

Vulnerability in Prayer

Like the father of the prodigal son, the Father longs to embrace, wash, and cleanse us of the stain of walking away from His perfect will. Forgiveness is a beautiful thing. So imperative to the gospel is forgiveness, and not just as a one-time event at salvation. We need washing from stumbling along the walk of life, even if our spirit was made righteousness at the acceptance of Christ's sacrifice for us in salvation. First John 1:9 explains, *"If we confess our sins, He is faithful and just to forgive us our sins and to cleanse us from all unrighteousness."*

Some have taught you don't need to confess sins, that it is all taken care of at salvation. If that is the case, I don't know why Jesus would teach in the Lord's Prayer, *"Forgive us our sins."* Jesus' model prayer contains confession; so should ours.

Daniel

Daniel modeled confession and repentance on behalf of others where their sin is affecting us. That is particularly true of ancestors and family members. Daniel, one of great integrity and righteousness, understood the prophecy of Jeremiah that there was to be 70 years of captivity. He set his heart to come before the Lord to pray for the accomplishment of that word.

> *Then I set my face toward the Lord God to make request by prayer and supplications, with fasting, sackcloth, and ashes. And I prayed to the Lord my God, and made confession and said, "...we have sinned and committed iniquity, we have done wickedly and rebelled, even by departing from Your precepts and Your judgments...We have not obeyed the voice of the Lord our God, to walk in His laws, which He set before us by His servants the prophets. Yes, all Israel has transgressed Your law, and has*

departed so as not to obey Your voice...O Lord, according to all Your righteousness, I pray, let Your anger and Your fury be turned away from Your city Jerusalem...O Lord, hear! O Lord, forgive!" (Daniel 9:3-19)

Stand in the Gap

God is looking for those willing to stand in the gap in prayer, willing to cry out in intercession and implore for forgiveness and mercy. Ezekiel 22:30 says, *"So I sought for a man among them who would make a wall, and stand in the gap before Me on behalf of the land, that I should not destroy it; but I found no one."* Unlike the day when Ezekiel recorded these words, may the Lord find those faithful in our day that will confess, repent and pray.

Years ago the Lord prompted me to repent on behalf of my ancestors, who are of Dutch heritage. Although I was born Canadian, both of my parents emigrated from Holland. I found a common saying in Holland was, "God made the world but the Dutch made Holland." That is related to the fact that the Dutch took land back from the sea, putting up dikes and expanding their landmass. It is also a sign of a pride and independence. The Netherlands means the "lowlands" and paradoxically, there is also a kind of low mentality, insecurity and "small" thinking. As I repented on behalf of my ancestors for such a mentality in my ancestry and in my own life, I felt the shift over myself and believe that repentance has positively affected my children.

PETITIONS

In the prayer Jesus uttered, recorded in John 17, He first prays for Himself, then for His disciples and lastly for all believers. The safety demonstrations on airplanes explain one must first put on their oxygen masks before assisting another. It is good to pray for yourself, petitioning the Father for things such as wisdom, health, provision, blessings on relationships, and the myriads of needs one may have. Then pray for those in your immediate sphere of influence: your spouse, children, extended family, friends, members of your church, and co-workers. Lastly, widen the prayers to those you may not personally know.

First John 5:15 states, *"And if we know that He hears us, whatever we ask, we know that we have the petitions that we have asked of Him."* God is a good God who answers prayers. We are not to be anxious or uptight about what will come or focus on problems. We are admonished to *"Be anxious for nothing, but in everything by prayer and supplication, with thanksgiving, let your requests be made known to God; and the peace of God, which surpasses all understanding, will guard your hearts and minds through Christ Jesus"* (Phil. 4:6-7).

Ruth Bell Graham

Ruth Bell Graham, the deceased wife of Billy Graham, used to use the daily newspaper as her prayer journal for that day. The needs in the nations are extensive. If you watch the news, turn it into quick prayer times for those involved in the many tragedies.

An attitude of "all we can do is pray" as some sort of last resort belittles the power of faith-filled prayers. The Lord has admonished me to not reach for the pain reliever if one of my children has a headache but to first pray. Make it the first line of offense and defense.

Chapter 3

PROPHETIC PRAYER

PROPHETIC DECREES

A simple definition for a prophetic decree would be "speaking in agreement with the Word and heart of God." This is where we purpose to fill our minds and mouths with the truth of the word of God, whether it is pure scripture or words He has spoken to us prophetically.

Joshua 1:8 states, *"This book of the Law shall not depart from your mouth, but you shall meditate in it day and night, that you may observe to do according to all that is written in it. For then you will make your way prosperous, and then you will have good success."* The Hebrew word meditate is *hagah*, meaning "to reflect, to ponder out loud to oneself." In Hebrew thought, to meditate upon the scriptures is to quietly repeat them in a soft, droning sound. Regular repetition of key scriptures and prophetic words will help create a womb for them to be accomplished in our lives and ministries.

And God Said...

How did God create the world? He spoke. What was utter void and emptiness shone out with light and substance at His word. Similarly, when we begin to declare with faith the words of God, they shift circumstances and obstacles around us. We are to call *"those things which do not exist as though they did"* (Rom. 4:17) and to speak to the mountain (obstacle) to be removed (see Matt. 17:20).

The Apostle Paul exhorted Timothy to wage war for the prophecies given over his life, to stir up the gift of God in him, and to not neglect the gift of God within him given by prophecy (see 1 Tim. 1:18, 2 Tim. 1:6, 1 Tim. 4:14). Paul knew the importance of taking faith-filled action as part of walking in fulfilled prophecy. Bill Johnson puts it this way, "Nothing happens in the Kingdom unless there is first a declaration."

Power of the Tongue

Proverbs 18:21 states, *"Death and life are in the power of the tongue, and those who love it will eat its fruit."* When we grasp just how important our words are in determining the course of our lives, it helps us not to frivolously toss them about like pebbles thrown in a pond. The ripple effect of our words can be far reaching. Matthew 12:36-37 says, *"But I say to you that for every idle word men may speak, they will give account of it in the day of judgment. For by your words you will be justified, and by your words you will be condemned."*

James 3 makes clear the power of the tongue, comparing it to a rudder in a ship or a bit in a horse's mouth. Such a small entity but oh, so powerful! You may recall from biology class the tongue has the most concentration of muscle mass of any body part. It may be small in size but powerful in impact—for good or bad.

When we use our agreement with God in spoken decrees, it has power to shift us as well as circumstances around us. Jesus did not model praying for miracles when He performed them; rather, He spoke for the miracle to happen. He knew His Father's will so he commanded the demon to leave, sickness to be healed, and the dead to rise. He decreed it, and so it was. When Jesus Himself was tempted by the devil, He quoted the Word of God resulting in the devil leaving and angels coming to minister to Him (see Matt. 4).

Regular declaration of words of life over your life, the lives of your family and loved ones, over your church, city and nation will bear significant fruit.

How to Decree

In order to actually do this, here are some helpful tips:

Be Consistent. Persistence in decrees is needed. When our youngest child, Glory Anna, was born with a protrusion in her mouth, we were told it was a *ranula* (problem with the salivary gland) and could only be repaired surgically, although it could wait a few years to be performed. We began to decree healing over our precious child who we did not want to see go through surgery. Four years later, the ranula suddenly disappeared one day. A consistent faith walk is needed.

Be Brief. In writing decrees, it is best to summarize the point in a sentence or two making it easier to actually decree regularly. For example, "I submit to God, draw near to Him, and walk in obedience," summarizes one desire of my heart.

Ensure the decrees are consistent with scripture and according to the nature of God. We want to ensure our declarations are in accord with the will of God. Decreeing a thing is not about us simply declaring we will receive our carnal desires that are not in accordance with God's heart for us. It's important that anything we decree is in line with the Word of God. One of my decrees is, "I live in perpetual, intimate communion with the Lord and have peace. His Presence is always with me." (See Matt. 28:20 and Phil. 4:7.)

Get Started. Write down three decrees of things prophesied over you that have not yet come to pass. Then write three decrees that declare the opposite of what you are struggling with. For example, if it is financial difficulty, call in breakthrough in this area (Prov. 10:22). Lastly, come up with three decrees of Godly desires you have. Begin to reshape your world through faith-filled alignment of your words with the heart of God for you and those around you.

Examples of Decrees

Here are some examples of daily decrees I use (more are included at the end of the section on Praying the Bible):

> "I am loved. The Lord loves me and is pleased with me. He calls me His delight, His treasure; His heart is ravished for me. I am accepted. I belong. I am significant."

> "I love the Lord with all my heart, soul, mind, and strength. I have passion for Jesus and am awakened in revelation about being His bride. The first commandment is my first priority."

> "I love people and I am loved by people. I walk in favor with God and man. I help prepare the Bride of Christ."

> "I fear no loss of anything God has given me. I am comforted by the assurance that God will intervene to give me protection and direction."

"God's goodness and mercy will continue all of our days. Therefore, I will prevail over failure, defeat and the attack of the enemy."

"The Lord is my shepherd, my leader, and my provider, who is responsible for me. I shall not lack anything that is needed in doing God's will in my life."

"Divinely endorse our lives."

"John and I and our family walk in great joy."

"The Lord has given me the spirit of wisdom and revelation in the knowledge of Him" (see Eph. 1:17).

"John and I have a deep, fantastic, intimate relationship and marriage. Our children are passionate lovers of God. They pursue the Lord; they live the Great Commandment and the Great Commission. They marry only the one the Lord has for them and they walk in fullness of destiny. Our children grow in favor with God and man. Doors from the Lord open for them. They are healthy."

(I have other specific declarations over myself, my husband, all of our six children, daughter-in-law, sons-in-law and three grandchildren).

PRAY THE BIBLE

Jeanne Guyon, in her classic book *Experiencing the Depths of Jesus Christ*, teaches on "beholding the Lord" through scripture. After reading a short passage of scripture, she teaches to pause in gentle quietness, setting your mind on the Spirit. Jeanne exhorts the reader to "set your mind inwardly, on Christ. The Lord is found only within your spirit, in the recesses of your being, in the Holy of Holies; this is where He dwells. The Lord once promised to come and make His home within you (see John 14:23). He promised to there meet those who worship Him and who do His will. The Lord will meet with you in your spirit. It was St. Augustine who once said that he had lost much time in the beginning of his Christian experience by trying to find the Lord outwardly rather than by turning inwardly."[14]

The written Word is to be a door through which we gain entry into the Living Word, Jesus Himself. Jesus was speaking to the religious leaders when He said in John 5:39-40, *"You search the Scriptures, for in them you think you have eternal life; and these are they which testify of Me. But you are not willing to come to Me that you may have life."* Notice Jesus is saying the words and letters of the scriptures themselves do not contain life, but it is coming to Him through the Word that produces life. We can come to Him and access Him through Spirit-inspired meditation and prayer of His Word.

Turn scripture passages into prayer. For example, if a particular verse admonishes us to obey, turn it into declarations such as, "I set my heart to obey you in this directive. Strengthen me to heed your words and build my life on the rock (see Matt. 7:24-29) of your commands." If a passage expresses a truth we are to believe, we can thank God for this truth and ask Him to reveal more of His heart to us as it pertains to that truth.

Make it Personal

Combining praying the Word with the concept of prophetic decrees, daily I will decree certain passages of scripture over myself or others, personalizing the passage. For example, using First Corinthians 13 as a personalized decree can look like, "I am patient and kind. I do not envy, parade myself, and am not puffed up. I do not behave rudely, do not seek my own, am not provoked and think no evil. I do not rejoice in iniquity, but rejoice in the truth. I bear all things, believe all things, hope all things, endure all things. Love never fails."

I pray the prayer of Jabez (see 1 Chron. 4:10) over every one of my family members inserting their names. I actually start my prayer time praying this prayer over my family and myself. I feel the anointing on it as I do so.

Our son is Judah, so for Judah, it goes like this, "Oh that You would bless Judah indeed and enlarge Judah's territory. That Your hand would be with Judah and that You would keep Judah from evil. That Judah may not cause pain."

More of my favorite scriptures to pray / declare are:

> *Let the words of my mouth and the meditation of my heart be acceptable in Your sight, Oh Lord, my strength and my Redeemer* (Psalm 19:14).

> *One thing I have desired of the Lord, that will I seek: That I may dwell in the house of the Lord all the days of my life, to behold the beauty of the Lord, and to inquire in His temple* (Psalm 27:4).

> *The Lord God has given me the tongue of the learned, that I should know how to speak a word in season to him who is weary. He awakens me morning by morning, He awakens my ear to hear as the learned. The Lord God has opened my ear; and I was not rebellious* (Isaiah 50:4-5).

> *The Lord will give strength to His people; the Lord will bless His people with peace* (Psalm 29:11).

"No weapon formed against you shall prosper, and every tongue which rises against you in judgment you shall condemn. This is the heritage of the servants of the Lord, and their righteousness is from Me," says the Lord (Isaiah 54:17).

Now to Him who is able to keep you from stumbling, and to present you faultless before the presence of His glory with exceeding joy (Jude 24).

Rejoice always, pray without ceasing, in everything give thanks; for this is the will of God in Christ Jesus for you (1 Thessalonians 5:16-18).

I have been crucified with Christ; it is no longer I who live, but Christ lives in me; and the life which I now live in the flesh I live by faith in the Son of God, who loved me and gave Himself for me (Galatians 2:20).

Now may He who supplies seed to the sower, and bread for food, supply and multiply the seed you have sown and increase the fruits of your righteousness (2 Corinthians 9:10).

You have put gladness in my heart (Psalm 4:7).

TONGUES

The mystery of speaking in tongues was revealed to me in my car. I had just left the home of a charismatic pastor I knew, and I was desperate to know the power of the Holy Spirit. At 19 years old, I was living at my parents' home on university summer break. Every night for three weeks in a row, at exactly 2 A.M., I was awakened by strange occurrences in my bedroom. I would see, with my natural eyes, figures such as a black-hooded faceless man standing next to my bed. I heard voices in my room and objects would mysteriously move, such as a candle that was knocked off a dresser and a poster that fell from my wall onto my bed. Needless to say, I was petrified; and although I would whisper the name of Jesus more in fear than in faith, I realized I did not have the kind of power or authority I read about in the book of Acts.

Two years earlier, I had received prayer for the baptism of the Holy Spirit. Nothing happened. I then believed a lie for two years that God must not want me to have this gift. Yet I read in the scriptures about being filled with the Holy Spirit and how easily believers received this infilling of the Spirit. The nightly torment was certainly convincing me of my need for the power of the Holy Spirit, and hence I sought out someone I knew who was of the charismatic persuasion. Upon receiving prayer from this pastor, I felt a fire permeate my body. But it wasn't until in the car on the drive home that the release of the gift of tongues poured forth from my lips. I was electric, ecstatic, and utterly convinced of the validity of this experience. I walked into my bedroom and commanded those tormenting spirits to leave in the name of Jesus. This time I felt full of faith, authority, and power. That night was the first night I slept through the night in three weeks. Ever since that time, three decades later, I have exercised the benefits of speaking and praying in tongues and have sought to pray for as many people as would like to receive the infilling of the Holy Spirit.

Scripture speaks of the phenomena of glossolalia as not speaking to men but in the spirit, speaking mysteries to God. Speaking in tongues edifies the person as opposed to prophecy, which edifies the church (see 1 Cor. 14:2,4).

There are actually two distinct ways of speaking in tongues: one as a form of prayer (see 1 Cor. 14:2,4,5,18) and the other as a prophetic utterance needing interpretation to be of any use to the general assembly of believers (see 1 Cor. 14:6-17,27-28).

Effects of Praying in Tongues

Many years ago I had a rare opportunity to minister to the broken addicts of Hong Kong with English missionary Jackie Pullinger. Jackie would constantly pray in tongues as she walked the city. When we arrived at an inner room in the notorious "Walled City" (a square block of depraved apartments, at that time not under jurisdiction by either the Chinese nor English governments; anarchy ruled, and it has since been demolished), I saw again and again drug addicts come to salvation, get filled with the Holy Spirit, and speak in tongues in a manner of mere minutes. Jackie would then get them off the streets to safe houses on surrounding islands, helping them to find new lives in Christ. Jackie taught on the power of a communion with the Holy Spirit in speaking in tongues. She found much greater effectiveness in her ministry as she daily practiced this gift.

Brain specialist Dr. Carl Peterson, M.D, conducted a study at Oral Roberts University, researching the brains of individuals who exercised glossolalia. It was discovered two chemical secretions in the brain are excreted only in the exercise of glossolalia—and in no other human activity. This secretion boosts the immune system 35 to 40 percent, promoting health and healing.[15]

The New York Times published findings of two studies of speaking in tongues. One was from researchers at the University of Pennsylvania, who took brain images of five women while they spoke in tongues. They found that their frontal lobes, which regulate thinking and through which people control what they do, were quiet as were the language centers. Dr. Andrew B. Newberg, leader of the study team, stated, "The amazing thing was how the images supported people's interpretation of what was happening. They way they describe it, and what they believe, is that God is talking through them." The article also quoted a study of nearly 1,000 evangelical Christians in England, finding that those who practice glossolalia were more emotionally stable than those who did not.[16]

A number of Christian leaders I know say they seek to practice speaking in tongues at least an hour a day. I personally seek to speak in tongues while driving my van, walking the dog, doing dishes, or in the house of prayer. I do feel encouraged and generally feel better after doing so as well as realizing I am communing and praying with the Holy Spirit in a way that may not be grasped by my mind, but is fully grasped by my spirit.

Chapter 4

THE POWER OF PRAYER

*D*aniel dedicated himself to fasting and prayer for 21 days. At the end of that time, an angel came to him to deliver a message. Recorded in Daniel 10, the angel explains the demonic power over the kingdom of Persia withheld this heavenly being until Michael, the archangel, came to war with those principalities enabling the breakthrough to get to Daniel with the message. The heavenly being says, *"Do not fear, Daniel, for from the first day that you set your heart to understand, and to humble yourself before your God, your words were heard; and I have come because of your words"* (Dan. 10:12). One man's words can cause the dispatching of angelic warriors and turn the course of life on planet earth. If that is possible through Daniel's words in prayer, it can be true of ours.

Faith-filled prayers change circumstances, move hearts, and accomplish great exploits. When we pray, there is an attraction of the angelic and a repulsion of the demonic. One word can sum up what prayer can do: *Anything*!

Hearing the stories of answered prayer helps to boost our faith and inspire us to press on in our prayer life. I never tire of hearing miracle stories of answered prayer.

ANSWERED PRAYER

My grandmother was a woman of prayer. Of her six children, five were believers, and two were ministers of the gospel. However, there was one prodigal son who refused to follow the ways of God. He married a non-Christian and for years lived outside of the saving knowledge of Jesus. Yet my grandmother never stopped praying for him. Year after year she implored Heaven for his salvation, petitioning God that even if it was not until his deathbed that the Lord would save him before he departed from earth. My grandmother went to Heaven without seeing the results of her prayers. Later, when my uncle was on his deathbed from cancer, he turned to Jesus and radically became a Christian. In fact, he lived two more years, attended church, and spoke of his salvation experience to others. My grandmother's prayers were heard and answered.

Ruth Bell Graham prayed fervently for their prodigal son, Franklin. Franklin, in his autobiography *Rebel with a Cause*, confesses he spent his late teens and early twenties running from God; smoking, drinking, getting bounced out of a Texas college, building homes for Eskimos in Alaska and spending his nights drinking shots and beers with "tough construction guys." Yet Franklin could not drown out the drawing of the Holy Spirit in response to his parents' faith-filled prayers. One night, in a hotel room in Jerusalem, Franklin turned to Jesus and underwent a life-altering conversion experience. Today, Franklin is a strong voice for truth, and serves as the president and CEO of the Billy Graham Evangelistic Association as well as leading the ministry Samaritan's Purse, an international Christian relief and evangelism organization.[17]

In the Bible

There are numerous biblical examples of the power of prayer. Let us look at just a few.

Moses interceded numerous times for the children of Israel while in the wandering wilderness years. The Lord heard and answered those prayers again and again. In the battle against the Amalekites in Exodus 17, Moses' intercession took on a strange form. When he held up his hands, Israel prevailed; and when he let down his hands, Amalek prevailed. Aaron and Hur came alongside to help Moses. One on each side, they held up his hands until the sun went down, and God granted Israel victory. This story is a good illustration of how the course of a battle can change due to one man standing in the gap, as well as how we need others to help stand with us in prayer.

The armies of Moab, Ammon, and Syria, a great multitude, were coming to battle against Jehoshaphat, the King of Judah, as recorded in Second Chronicles 20. Fearing defeat, Jehoshaphat interceded to the Lord, *"For we have no power against this great multitude that is coming against us; nor do we know what to do, but our eyes are upon You"* (1 Chron. 20:12). Jahaziel then prophesied, *"Thus says the Lord to you: 'Do not be afraid nor dismayed because of this great multitude, for the battle is not yours, but God's'"* (1 Chron. 20:15). The Bible goes on to say:

> *And Jehoshaphat bowed his head with his face to the ground, and all Judah and the inhabitants of Jerusalem bowed before the Lord, worshiping the Lord…And when he had consulted with the people, he appointed those who should sing to the Lord, and who should praise the beauty*

of holiness, as they went out before the army and were saying: "Praise the Lord, for His mercy endures forever." Now when they began to sing and to praise, the Lord set ambushes against the people of Ammon, Moab, and Mount Seir, who had come against Judah; and they were defeated (1 Chronicles 20:18,21-22).

What an incredible example of the power of prayer and praise and the resulting power of God poured out.

Just prior to Jesus' ascension, He instructed His followers to tarry in Jerusalem until they were endued with the power of the Holy Spirit (see Luke 24:49). After ten days of pressing in, there were 120 of the believers gathered together in the upper room praying with one accord when there came the sound of a mighty rushing wind, and the appearance of tongues of fire as the Holy Spirit was poured out in power at Pentecost (see Acts 2).

The disciples encountered various types of persecution from the Roman Empire or religious leaders. In Acts 4:29-31 they prayed, *"Now, Lord, look on their threats, and grant to Your servants that with all boldness they may speak Your word, by stretching out Your hand to heal, and that signs and wonders may be done through the name of Your holy Servant Jesus. And when they had prayed, the place where they were assembled together was shaken; and they were all filled with the Holy Spirit, and they spoke the word of God with boldness."* They saw an immediate answer to their faith-filled prayers.

Around the World

Throughout history, God has remained actively involved in the lives of His people answering prayers.

When we were in Germany recently, we learned how during the 1980s, there was a group of believers in a city of eastern Germany praying and crying out for the end of Communist rule, as were others around the world. In November of 1989, a restriction was lifted where East Germans were allowed to visit West Germany after a quarter of a century of being separated by the barrier wall. As they came in droves to visit West Germany, both East and West Germans began to chip away at the wall, which was later completely torn down. Communism in Germany was abolished. It happened suddenly for those of us viewing from the west, but it was an answer to fervent and consistent prayer.

Rees Howells

Rees Howells was a man who lived in Wales and was deeply affected by the Welsh Revival of the early 1900s. He was at first a coal miner who the Lord called to become a missionary to South Africa. Revival came to South Africa due to this man's prayers as recounted in this account: "While on their knees in prayer, the Lord spoke to Mr. Howells, telling him that their prayer was heard and revival was coming. They waited and then He came. In the meeting, the whole congregation was on their faces crying out to God." Like lightning and thunder, the power came. "You can never describe those meetings when the Holy Spirit comes down," wrote Rees Howells.[18]

Rees went on to found a Bible school and children's home in Wales, with no money or job to his name. However, he had the power of prayer, and the Lord answered by abundantly providing for these buildings.[19]

Another battle of intercession concerned the German air raids in 1940, and the crises of the Battle of Britain. German Army General Goering made his great attempt to gain mastery of the air in preparation for the invasion of England. At the same time, the church was praying fervently, led in intercession by Rees Howells. On September 15, 1940 Winston Churchill gives this account in his war memoirs. He visited the operations room of the RAF that day and watched as the enemy squadrons poured in, and the Royal Air Force went out to meet them.

Churchill asked his air marshall, "What other reserves have we?" "There are none," the man answered, and reported how grave Mr. Churchill looked. Then another five minutes passed and "it appeared that the enemy were going home. The shifting of the discs on the table showed a continuous eastward movement of the German bombers and fighters. No new attack appeared. In another ten minutes the action was ended." There seemed no reason why the Luftwaffe should have turned for home, just at the moment when victory was in their grasp.

After the war Air Chief Marshall Lord Dowding, Commander in chief of Fighter command in the Battle of Britain, made this statement: "Even during the battle one realized from day to day how much external support was coming in. At the end of the battle one had the sort of feeling that there had been some special Divine intervention to alter some sequence of events which would have otherwise occurred."[20]

Churchill himself, speaking of the RAF, said, "Never before has so much been owed by so many to so few." Churchill was speaking of the Air Force, and yet that statement can also apply to the intercessors praying for deliverance. Never had so much been owed by so many in the nation and the world to the few who were willing to press into prayer.

FASTING

The practice of regular fasting, as normal Christian behavior, was taught by Jesus, exercised by the early church (see Matt. 6:16-17; 9:15; Acts 13:2), and has been the regular discipline of believers throughout church history. The practice of fasting in scripture usually includes, but is not limited to, abstinence from food, and may be engaged in for varying durations, typically for no more than a few days at a time.

Arthur Wallis, in his book *God's Chosen Fast*, said, "Fasting… opens the way for the outpouring of the Spirit and the restoration of God's house. Fasting in this age of the absent Bridegroom is in expectation of His return. Soon there will be the midnight cry, 'Behold the bridegroom! Come out to meet him.' It will be too late then to fast and to pray. The time is now."[21]

Basil, Bishop of Caesarea (AD 330-379) said, "Fasting begets prophets and strengthens strong men. Fasting makes lawgivers wise; it is the soul's safeguard, the body's trusted comrade, the armor of the champion, the training of the athlete."[22] Jesus said in Matthew 9:15, *"But the days will come when the Bridegroom will be taken away from them, and then they will fast."*

Fasting Guidelines

Fasting is always voluntary and the individual in consultation with the Lord should determine the length and nature of the fast. Leaders may invite others to join in a corporate fast; but again, it should always be voluntary. Corporate fasting may be for a specific time and with a specific goal in mind. It can be powerful in the context of unity and commitment to prayer and to the Word (see Joel 2:15). John and I usually call a 40-day fast for our church at the beginning of each year, and people join in, as they feel called and able. Even the children may fast ice cream or chocolate, and the teens might fast social media or movies.

While the physical impact of fasting is real, the spiritual benefits of fasting are undeniable. Any fast undertaken must be done with spiritual wholeheartedness and wisdom in dealing with our physical body. For example, pregnant women, nursing mothers and children should not fast from food for physical and medical reasons. One of our daughters fasted so extensively as a teenager, it seemed to cause her thyroid function to destabilize for a period of time. However, while 16 years old, she fasted movies for a whole year and that proved to be a more fruitful fast for her and she tremendously grew spiritually that year.

A "Fasted Lifestyle"

A "fasted lifestyle" is a disciplined lifestyle, in which we steward our bodies and time with wisdom and diligence. Fasting is not only abstention; it is an exchange where we abstain from certain things in order to "feast" on God's Word and prayer, whereby the abundance of His grace is made more readily available to us. When undertaken with this type of commitment, a fasted lifestyle is sustainable on a long-term basis, just as it was for Daniel and his friends (see Dan. 1).

Some different fasts include a Daniel fast (eating vegetables and water), a fruit and vegetable fast, a juice fast, or a water-only fast. Esther called for a total fast for a period of three days (this one can be very physically taxing and should not be undertaken for longer than three days); some people may fast meats and sweets, or fast other "comforts" in the physical such as Internet, social media, TV or movies.

Target of Fasting

It is helpful to have a clear target as your prayer focus while you fast. Personally, it may pertain to a financial or healing need. Corporately, it could be praying for revival, for prodigal sons and daughters to come to Jesus, or for a corporate breakthrough in warfare over the enemy's plans.

We are told to not boast about fasting and only let others know as is necessary (see Matt. 6:16-18). Daniel prepared himself to receive revelation through fasting (see Dan. 10:1-2) and there is reward for fasting (Matt. 6:18) so we can expect to receive revelation, and hear God's voice.

While You Fast

When John and I began to regularly fast, we noticed we would become grumpy. At first I thought, "Oh, that's just because we are fasting." However, the Lord spoke to me and showed me fasting does tend to bring up the things that are not right in us. Indeed we detox, not just physically but spiritually in a fast. In other words, He was telling me if grumpiness is coming up, it is because it was in me and needed to go. Once we got breakthrough in that area (or cleansed of it), we found we did not become grumpy in fasting.

Prepare for opposition in fasting. The day of your fast donuts may be brought into your office, your mother makes your favorite meal, or suddenly you are invited out to eat. Satan tempted Jesus while He was fasting and we can expect the same. Seek to press through, stand in your victory, and follow through with your commitment of fasting before the Lord. If you do fail, don't give into condemnation. God always extends grace. Just hit the "delete" button and continue on in your fast.

Lastly, breakthroughs often come after a fast, not during it. Do not listen to the lie that nothing is happening. Every fast, done in faith, will be rewarded.

PRAYER EVANGELISM

As Jesus instructed his disciples, the best way to evangelize is to first pray. *"Then He said to His disciples, 'The harvest truly is plentiful, but the laborers are few. Therefore pray the Lord of the harvest to send out laborers into His harvest'"* (Matt. 9:37-38). We have found much greater effectiveness in soul winning since we began regular prayer for the prodigals to come home to the Father and the lost to be saved.

Ed Silvoso, a revivalist and evangelist originally from Argentina, has seen cities turn to the saving knowledge of Jesus as Savior. His book, *That None Should Perish*, is excellent. Simply put, prayer evangelism, he says, is "talking to God about our neighbors before we talk to our neighbors about God." With the backing of experience, Ed teaches that the spiritual climate of a region is changed through prayer.

Lighthouses of Prayer

Ed encourages lighthouses of prayer in neighborhoods all over a city, which are gatherings of one or more people in Jesus' name for the purpose of praying for, caring for, and sharing Jesus Christ with their neighbors and those in their sphere of influence. The primary purpose of a lighthouse is to establish the Presence of Jesus in every neighborhood, office, school, and workplace.

A lighthouse of prayer may be a family praying for their neighbors, a schoolteacher praying for their pupils and their families, a receptionist praying for the people in their office, or a store employee praying for the people in their department.

Ed teaches,

> The way that you become a lighthouse is to stand on your front porch and count five neighbors on your right—if you live on a corner, just keep counting, going around the corner, count five neighbors on your left, pick the house directly across from you and five on each side of that house, and begin praying for them.
>
> You can do this in any place—it could be apartments instead of houses, school lockers, your teammates, five desks on either side of yours at work, or in school.

I would do this where you most relate to non-Christians. If your primary relationships with unbelievers are in you workplace, school, children's day-care, start there. I will talk mostly of neighbors, but take the most natural group for you to relate to.[23]

Four Principles of Evangelism

Ed teaches four principles of prayer evangelism based on Luke 10:5,8-9: *"Whatever house you enter, first say, 'Peace be to this house'… Whatever city you enter, and they receive you, eat such things as are set before you. And heal the sick there, and say to them, 'The Kingdom of God has come near to you.'"*

From this passage, the four principles are: speak peace to them, fellowship with them, take care of their needs, and proclaim the good news.

Speaking peace to our neighbors means blessing them; stop complaining about them in our hearts (possibly due to judgments in our hearts towards those living unredeemed lives), and pray for the blindness on them to be broken. *"The god of this world has blinded the minds of the unbelievers, to keep them from seeing the light of the gospel of the glory of Christ"* (2 Cor. 4:4, ESV).

Blessing the lost opens the doors to fellowship and fellowship leads to opportunities to meet their felt needs. This will happen only after they trust us enough to disclose those needs. Once such trust exists, they may share that their marriage is in trouble, that they fear losing their job or may need help to overcome an addiction. We can then pray for them regarding those needs and when they see those prayers answered, they will be more inclined to realize they need salvation.

HINDRANCES TO PRAYER

There can be hindrances to our prayer life. If we are aware of them, it can help us resist these potential blockades.

Demonic Resistance

First of all, there is a very real battle in the spirit realm with demonic spirits seeking to keep us from praying. C.S. Lewis in his classic book, *The Screwtape Letters*, tells of fictitious letters from a higher-ranking demon to a lower-ranking demon on how to carry out their dark plans. In one letter he writes on the need to destroy prayer saying, "Interfere at any price in any fashion when people start to pray, for real prayer is lethal to our cause."[24]

Willful Sin

Willful sin in one's life can hinder our prayer lives in that sin tends to drive us away from, rather than toward God. Psalm 66:18 states, *"If I regard iniquity in my heart, the Lord will not hear."* Personal integrity and character are sure foundations for a powerful life of prayer. As a man is, so he prays. He cannot be shallow and frivolous by nature and yet pray with depth and intensity. I have heard it said this way, "It is as men live that they pray. It is the life that prays."

Excuses

We can have myriads of excuses that arise, hindering our prayer. Maybe we are too busy, don't have enough time, are too tired to arise early to pray, or there are too many other priorities that take precedence over a life of prayer. Dick Eastman said this, "In this restless and busy age most of us live too much in public. We spend our spiritual strength and forget to renew it. We multiply engagements and curtail our prayers. By an error of judgment, or perhaps by the subtle force of inclination, which we mistake for necessity, we work when we ought to pray because to an active mind work is far easier than prayer."[25] Martin Luther said, "Work, work, and more work from early until late. In fact, I have so much to do that I shall spend the first three hours in prayer."[26] He knew that prayer paves the way for accomplishment.

Lack of Perseverance

Another temptation is to give up too quickly and not persist in prayer as mentioned earlier. Instead of a mentality of instant results, we need a spirit of endurance as it pertains to our prayer life.

Some great news is Jesus lives to make intercession for us. As we come to Him for help, He enables us to overcome every hurdle and hindrance in prayer as well as in life.

Chapter 5

THE HOUSE OF PRAYER

*I*n early 2003, I walked outside my suburban Toronto home to see a little praying mantis (a green insect with its "hands" raised in a prayer position) on my doorstep. In fact, it was at my doorstep every morning for three weeks. I began to wonder if God was trying to get my attention, as one doesn't normally find praying mantises in the midst of the city.

By September of that year, our family moved to a city over an hour drive from Toronto to assume a senior pastorate position at a church connected with the Toronto church. We realized the church needed a lot of divine help to repair wounds in the hearts of people, reclaim the place of the Presence of God, and see hearts transformed. In fact the city had problems with drug addiction, including among high school students. I discovered that the city streets were founded on the freemasonry symbol, and I felt a head pain, like a band around my head, when entering the borders of the city.

John and I had just left Toronto as associate pastors. The Toronto church was in revival, where the Presence of God was so strong and God moved powerfully. We knew we could not regress to dead, dull, boring church. We desperately needed a breakthrough from God, so we set ourselves to pray.

As we sought the Lord, He spoke to us. One of the first things God said was, "I do not send you to war to lose. I send you out to war to win." It was a mentality shift from negativity to victory. We needed to believe, to have faith. Secondly, the Lord said to worship, pray, and declare that He was Lord of that city. He admonished us to give our weekday mornings to Him in prayer. Since there was a great Christian school in that city, for that season we stepped out of homeschooling our children, put them in school and John and I set aside 8–11:30 A.M. to pray and seek the Lord. At first it was pure obedience as we sought the Lord together in prayer, not necessarily feeling a big anointing on our prayer times. I would get out my guitar, and we worshipped and prayed together.

Then the Lord said to move the location of our newly formed prayer meeting to the church. Others began to join us in prayer and worship.

TEACH, LIVE, AND DO THE TABERNACLE

One day while I was seeking the Lord personally, the tangible Presence of the Lord filled the room. I got down on my knees knowing something important and supernatural was happening. I heard the voice of the Holy Sprit speak clearly to me, "I want you to teach, live, and do the Tabernacle of David." In my mind, I thought, "What is the Tabernacle of David?" However, audibly I said to the Lord through my tears, "Yes Lord." I did not realize the specifics of what was to come but I did know there was great significance to this message. Hence, I began to study the Tabernacle of David from the scriptures, from books and any source I could find. As we will see, the Tabernacle of David is very relevant for today.

Even before we started the House of Prayer, we had a prophetic word from a visiting speaker. He prophesied that something was about to be birthed in our city and in our church that was eventually going to go to Toronto. "And as a sign this is a word from the Lord," he said, "if you investigate it, a river flows from here to Toronto." Sure enough, after investigation, there was a river that flowed the 150 kilometers from our city to Toronto. We would not know the fulfillment of that word until eight years had passed.

Visiting the International House of Prayer in Kansas City (IHOP-KC), which has been operating in continuous night and day worship and prayer since September of 1999, inspired us greatly. We could tangibly feel the Presence of God in their midst, something we desired greatly. We continued to build the House of Prayer in our own city with more and more people coming to attend, including musicians, singers, intercessors, and worship leaders. The path of the House of Prayer in our city took various turns as the Lord led us. We received teaching on the "harp and bowl" model and began to incorporate the worship and prayer format in our House of Prayer. For nine months we moved the location of the prayer to a downtown storefront facility, and went 24 hours a day with many from other churches in the city joining us.

The Shift Begins

Meanwhile, in our church, the first indication something was shifting as a result of answered prayer was when prodigal sons and daughters of people in our congregation came to radical salvation. They got free of addictions, turned to Jesus, and many became great examples of godly youth. The Presence of God increased in our midst. An anointing of the prophetic was released, worship teams became more anointed, people began to be healed, and the church grew numerically. We stared an internship program in response to requests from young adults wanting to come and join us in the work in our city. They would come after graduating from different schools of ministry or Bible schools, such as the Catch the Fire School of Ministry in Toronto, the Bethel School of Supernatural Ministry in California, IHOP-KC's One Thing Internships, or various Bible schools. That initially surprised us, as we wondered why young people would want to come from various countries around the world to our relatively small city. Yet their lives were being impacted; they grew in ministry gifting and were a tremendous help in the House of Prayer as well as in the life of the church.

Simultaneously, within our city, a seedy hotel known for drug deals burned to the ground. Drug houses started to be discovered by police or would mysteriously blow up. Strangely, the top drug dealer to the high schools came to church one day. He was overcome by the conviction of the Holy Spirit, initially going to the men's restroom to compose himself. When he came back into the service, I was speaking a message on the judgment seat of Christ. That man gave his life to Jesus and repented of his drug-dealing ways, which removed a main drug source in our city.

Prayer in the City

My husband became the President of the Council of Churches and started a smaller prayer meeting weekly among some of the pastors. Unity grew between congregations of life-giving ministries and even some citywide endeavors arose with churches working together.

The mayor of the city contacted my husband requesting help to start a mayor's prayer breakfast. We hadn't thought of that but it sounded like a great idea, so the Annual Mayor's Prayer Breakfast was born with 300 of the city's top business, political, and church leaders attending to hear Christian songs sung, biblical passages read, and inspiring messages given. A flyer distributed from the mayor's office during some of those events had the city emblem on the front and the word written inside, "Jesus Christ is Lord." We wondered how many cities in the world actually acknowledged Jesus as Lord from the office of the mayor. Indeed, a shift was happening in our midst. Those who were involved in the House of Prayer felt the direct connection to answered prayer.

House of Prayer, Toronto

In 2011, the doors opened to return to Toronto as the Campus Pastors of Catch the Fire Toronto Airport and to start the House of Prayer. The prophecy about God birthing something that was going to go to Toronto came to pass. It was the House of Prayer with regular, corporate prayer and worship.

The House of Prayer at Catch the Fire in Toronto operates today at 20 hours a week and in addition, one all-night prayer and worship the first Friday of a month. The Presence of God has increased in our midst. God is moving in response to regular, corporate prayer and worship.

E.M. Bounds stated, "The preaching man is to be the praying man. Prayer is to be the preachers best weapon."[27] Rev. Mark Pearse puts it this way, "The prayer meeting is the thermometer of the church. It tests what degree of warmth there is. The prayer meeting is the barometer of the church and points to showers of blessings or seasons of drought."[28] Church achievements are directly related to its corporate prayer life. By extension, the prayer life of the church will be related to the prayer life of the pastor or apostolic leader.

THE HOUSE OF PRAYER

Scriptures recounts a time when Jesus was very angry. In fact, He overturned tables sending coins sprawling and forced out of the temple those there for reasons centered on money. He declared, *"It is written, 'My house shall be called a house of prayer,' but you have made it a 'den of thieves'"* (Matt. 21:13). Jesus was quoting Isaiah 56:7, which also states the Lord would make them *"joyful in My house of prayer,"* and it was to be a house of prayer *"for all nations."* Obviously, the temple at that time was not exemplifying the heart of God to be a place of joy and prayer.

What is the "House of Prayer"?

So what is the House of Prayer? What was Jesus talking about? And how does this tie into the Tabernacle of David?

In short, the focus of the temple was to be on the centrality of the majesty, worth, worship, and prayer to the one true God. The religious leaders of Jesus' day had gotten off into other temporal, even contrary priorities. I have wondered what Jesus would do if He walked into the churches of today. Are the houses of the Lord today living out His mandate that *"My house shall be a house of prayer for all nations"*? Perhaps some are and some are not.

David and the Ark

David was a man after God's own heart. In a desperate state, recorded in Psalm 132:3-5, David made what some call the "vow that changed history": *"Surely I will not go into the chamber of my house, or go up to the comfort of my bed; I will not give sleep to my eyes or slumber to my eyelids, until I find a place for the Lord, a dwelling place for the Mighty One of Jacob."* David could not go about ordinary life until there was a breakthrough in the Presence of God in their midst. He had finally become king of all of Israel and among his first priorities was to put the worship of God center stage.

To this end, David went after the embodiment of the glory of God in that day, the Ark of the Covenant. The Philistines in the battle with Israel had captured the Ark, the same day the priest Eli and his two sons died. When Eli's daughter-in-law, heavy with child, heard the news that the Ark was captured and her husband and father-in-law had died, she entered into labor, gave birth to a son, and named him Ichabod, meaning "inglorious." She said, *"The glory has departed from Israel!"* (1 Sam. 4:22).

The Philistines and the Ark

The Philistines initially put the Ark in the temple of their god, Dagon. Yet each morning, the statue of Dagon would be found fallen on its face before the Ark, and subsequently the head and hands broke off this statue of their false god (see 1 Sam. 5:2-4). When they broke out in tumors, the Philistines realized God was against them and they sought to return the Ark to Israel. How did they do this? By putting it on a new cart pulled by milk cows whose calves they removed from them. Their experiment was if these cows went of their own volition to the land of Israel, it was a confirmation the God of Israel had brought the destruction on them (see 1 Sam. 6).

I was raised on a farm and milked cows as I grew up. I know what it is like to separate a cow from its calf. The cow will make every effort to be reunited. The Bible says the cows went straight for the land of Israel, lowing as they went. I remember the deep, sound of a cow lowing for its calf. It is a disturbing sound. This bit of biblical trivia shows the power of God contained in that Ark and the ways He wanted it back in the hands of His people. Yet the Ark sat neglected for some 70 years—until David.

David went to the house of Abinadab in Kirjath Jearim to obtain the Ark but initially did the transport incorrectly, on a cart pulled by oxen. I have stood on the hill of Kirjath Jearim in Israel looking toward Jerusalem. There are steep hills to descend and ascend in the journey, and the oxen stumbled on one of the hills near a threshing floor. Uzzah (one of the 30,000 choice men David brought with him to transport the Ark) stretched out his hand to steady the Ark and was struck dead immediately by the Lord. David was both angry and afraid of the Lord and asked, *"How can the ark of the Lord come to me?"* (2 Sam. 6:9). David turned aside and put the Ark in the home of Obed-Edom, the Gittite.

Obed-Edom

David's question is a very important, valid question. It can be paraphrased, "How do I effectively get the glory of God in my midst?" The proper protocol in transporting the Ark was to have it carried on the shoulders of the priests. It was God's people, called to minister to Him, who were to bring in the glory. Remember the discussion of who are today's priests? We are! Who helps bring in the glory of God? We do! How? Well, let us continue with the story of David.

The Ark was in the home of Obed-Edom for three months and the Lord blessed him and his household in that time. David then returned for the Ark to transport it the six miles to Jerusalem. In his extravagance and radical love for the Lord, David had the priest stop every six steps along the way to make a sacrifice to the Lord (see 2 Sam. 6:13). Theologians have estimated that to be 2,437 stops. Assuming at least 30 minutes to make a sacrifice to the Lord and including any sleep time, it would have taken 100 days to journey the six miles. Additionally, David danced before the Lord with all of his might as they entered with the Ark into Jerusalem, setting it in the tabernacle David had erected for it.

David Worships the Lord

David wore a linen ephod as he danced and transported the Ark—the attire supposedly only to be worn by priests. David was foreshadowing the day when the priestly role to minister to the Lord would be broader than the tribe of Levites but rather to all who would love the Lord with all of their hearts. Second Samuel 6:18 states, *"And when David had finished offering burnt offerings and peace offerings, he blessed the people in the name of the Lord of hosts."* David modeled the priestly before the kingly role. First bless and minister to the Lord (priest), then you can go into the outer court and minster to the people (king). Keep the order of priority correct and you will be blessed and be a blessing. I've heard it said David was a radical lover of God, whose side job was to be the king of Israel.

David's wife Michal, daughter of Saul, challenged David about his dancing before the maidservants, wearing nothing but an ephod. But David saw beyond her question to reveal her heart and responded, *"It was before the Lord, who chose me instead of your father and all his house, to appoint me ruler over the people of the Lord, over Israel. Therefore I will play music before the Lord. And I will be even more undignified than this, and will be humble in my own sight"* (2 Sam. 6:21-22). Saul was the first king of Israel, but it didn't seem to cross his mind to bring the Ark into a place of prominence, centering the kingdom around the worship of the Lord. It took David to usher in this era.

THE TABERNACLE OF DAVID

David's Tabernacle took a very different form than the Tabernacle of Moses. The Tabernacle of Moses had the outer court, inner court, and the Hholy of Holies, and was very somber and solemn in tone. There was no sound or music. The High Priest would alone go into the Holy of Holies and see the Ark of the Covenant, bringing sacrifice for the atonement for the sins of the people and that would be only once a year. By contrast, the Tabernacle of David did not have the divisions of rooms, had much sound, and many could see and worship before the Lord at the Ark of the Covenant.

David erected a tent over the ark and established continuous night and day worship and prayer before the Lord. His tabernacle had music, clapping, dancing, antiphonal singing, singing of the scriptures, intercession, thankfulness, rejoicing, lifting up hands, shouting, psalms, joy-filled praise, seeking, and ministering to the Lord (see 1 Chron. 15, 16). For the first time in scripture, music is equated with or added to worship.

Out of 38,000 Levitical priests, David established 24,000 to look after the work of the House of the Lord; 6,000 were to be officers and judges; 4,000 of them were gatekeepers; and 4,000 worshipped the Lord with musical instruments that David made (see 1 Chron. 23:3-5, 7). In addition, there were 288 prophetic singers (see 1 Chron. 25:6) and David put a great deal of money into the work of the House of the Lord. The Lord had commanded Israel to financially support the singers and musicians, who stood before the Lord.

Theologians estimate that the Tabernacle of David continued non-stop for between 33 to 40 years. It coincides with Israel's greatest time of blessing, greatest boundaries in history, and peace was established all around. I have heard it said that Israel's greatest time in worship coincided with its broadest boundaries in government, and David led both.

Old Testament Revivals of the Tabernacle of David

When one reads the books of Kings and Chronicles, you can discern a pattern. When the Hebrew people would turn away from the Lord in disobedience, worship false gods, or neglect the law of the Lord, the Lord would allow enemy armies to rise up against them. If they turned to the Lord in repentance, the Lord would deliver them. There are revivals recorded in the Old Testament where the leadership restored Davidic worship, putting the singers and musicians in place to worship the Lord.

Five generations after David, around 870 BC, King Jehoshaphat led a reform, which included establishing singers and musicians to praise the Lord (see 2 Chron. 20:19-28). Jehoshaphat learned the battle strategy of worship and prayer. Later, King Jehoiada restored temple worship in the order of David around 835 BC (see 2 Chron. 23:18).

King Hezekiah's revival about 725 BC included restoring singers and musicians as David commanded (see 2 Chron. 29:25-27). King Josiah's revival of righteousness in 625 BC restored full-time singers and musicians as David had commanded (see 2 Chron. 35:3-15).

After the children of Israel were captured and taken to Babylon, the Persian King Cyrus was stirred by the Lord to proclaim the captives could return to the land of Israel and begin to rebuild. Jeremiah prophesied this some 100 years before (see 2 Chron. 36:22-23) even giving Cyrus' name. Zerubbabel led the first wave of exiles returning to Jerusalem to rebuild the temple, around 536 BC, taking 200 singers and musicians with him (see Ezra 2:65).

Zerubbabel established full-time singers and musicians as commanded by David (see Ezra 3:10-11).

Ezra led a second wave of exiles back to Israel around 458 BC and helped lead a spiritual reformation. Nehemiah, cupbearer to King Artaxerxes, came to help rebuild the walls around Jerusalem in 445 BC. Together Ezra and Nehemiah helped reestablish full-time singers and musicians as commanded by David (see Neh. 12:24,45). Nehemiah was instrumental in ensuring the singers and musicians were financially supported and did not have to go back to the work in the fields (see Neh. 13:5,10-12).

In the next chapter we will see how this extraordinary prayer movement initiated by God and implemented by King David not only weaves throughout biblical and church history, but also is experiencing a phenomenal resurgence in this day and hour.

Chapter 6

PRAYER IN THE NEW TESTAMENT AND BEYOND

NEW TESTAMENT CORPORATE PRAYER

As noted before, Jesus modeled a devout prayer life, likewise teaching His disciples to pray.

The early church embraced a lifestyle of personal and corporate prayer. In a prayer meeting, they tarried to receive the promise of the Spirit (see Acts 2:1-4) and they *"continued with one accord in prayer and supplication"* (Acts 1:14). It was the disciples' custom to come to the temple at the *"hour of prayer"* (Acts 3:1). The early church continued daily with one another in one accord in the temple (see Acts 2:46) and not just in homes. Many chapters in the book of Acts recount corporate prayer meetings. It was a part of the early church's culture.

The order of worship that God commanded David to embrace is timeless. Next we will turn to church history.

CHURCH HISTORY

Throughout history, the Lord has always had at least a remnant of radical lovers of His heart, pressing into prayer. This is by no means an exhaustive list but here are some examples of persistent prayer.

In 555 AD in Bangor, Ireland a prayer movement began composed of some 3,000 monks, led by Comgall and Columbanus. One-third of the community would take eight-hour shifts of prayer, reading the scriptures and worship leading to worship and prayer 24 hour a day for 300 years. This community sent out missionaries with apostolic power, starting churches, educational centers and spreading revival throughout Europe. The Roman Empire fell during this time.[29]

In Clairvaux, France around 1120 AD, Bernard and his 700 monks gathered to pray. This continued day and night for many years, resulting in a dynamic release of evangelism through signs and wonders across Europe.[30]

Moravian Revival

Count Zinzendorf was a wealthy landowner, born into nobility in what is now known as Germany. He was also a radical man of God. In 1722 Zinzendorf offered asylum on his estate to persecuted believers from Moravia and Bohemia (parts of Czech Republic). They built a community called Herrnhut. Initially the community ran into various conflicts and relational problems until persistent prayer began around 1727 AD. Continuous worship and intercession continued for 120 years resulting in the sending forth of missionaries around the world.

The famous story that has inspired many in the missions movement for over 250 years occurred in December of 1732 when Leonard Dober and David Nitschmann, both in their early twenties, were sent out as the first two Moravian missionaries. They departed from Herrnhut for St. Thomas Island in the West Indies. Once there, they sold themselves into slavery to reach the 3,000 slaves who worked the sugarcane fields owned by an atheist landowner, who had vowed never to allow Christianity to reach his property. As they departed on a ship from Hamburg to sail through the North Sea, their families, knowing they would likely never see them again, wept as they asked them why they must go. One of them cried out what became the banner call for all Moravian missionaries, "May the Lamb that was slain receive the reward of His sufferings."

Over the next 150 years, the Moravians sent out 2,000 missionaries to neglected areas of the earth such as the West Indies, Greenland, to the North American Indians, Livonia, the shores of the Baltic Sea, the slaves of South Carolina, Suriname, to the slaves of several parts of South America, to the Copts of Egypt, the Inuit of Labrador, and to the west coast of South Africa.[31,32]

The Church Today

David Yonggi Cho founded Yoido Full Gospel Church in Seoul, Korea, the world's largest church of nearly one million members. He also founded Prayer Mountain, and prayer meetings that have continued continuously night and day since 1973. Cho's ministry has thousands of prayer cells. Asked the reason for this kind of growth in a New York magazine interview, Rev. Cho declared, "We are a praying people."[33]

The International House of Prayer in Kansas City, under the leadership of Mike Bickle, has been forging continuous night and day prayer and worship since September of 1999. The ministry has expanded to various internships, children, youth and adult teaching schools, as well as a university known as International House of Prayer University.

HARP AND BOWL

King David combined worship with prayer in the Tabernacle of David, which also appears to be Heaven's model.

> *Now when He had taken the scroll, the four living creatures and the twenty-four elders fell down before the Lamb, each having a harp, and golden bowls full of incense, which are the prayers of the saints. And they sang a new song, saying: "You are worthy to take the scroll, and to open its seals; for You were slain, and have redeemed us to God by Your blood out of every tribe and tongue and people and nation, and have made us kings and priests to our God; and we shall reign on the earth. Then I looked, and I heard the voice of many angels around the throne, the living creatures, and the elders; and the number of them was ten thousand times ten thousand, and thousands and thousands, saying with a loud voice: Worthy is the Lamb who was slain to receive power and riches and wisdom, and strength and honor and glory and blessing!"* (Revelation 5:8-12)

The "harp" signifies worship (agreeing with who God is, loving God) and the "bowl" speaks of intercession (agreeing with what God wants to do, loving others). Besides being Heaven's model, what are some reasons to embrace the harp and bowl, or worship with intercession, model of corporate prayer?

Reasons to Embrace This Model

Isaiah 56:7 states, *"I will...make them joyful in My house of prayer."* There is greater joy in prayer when we add worship, causing the heart to awaken to the beauty of God. An awakened, fascinated heart equals more joy-filled times of prayer. E.M. Bounds said, "Prayer should not be regarded as a duty which must be performed, but rather as a privilege to be enjoyed, a rare delight that is always revealing some new beauty."[34]

A prophetic spirit is cultivated in the musicians and singers as they play before the Lord in worship and intercession. This helps to cultivate a vibrant spiritual atmosphere in the church. The prophetic brings life as the Holy Spirit speaks. Worship stirs up the prophetic (see 1 Chron. 25:1-3; 2 Kings 3:15). Intimacy with the beautiful God is enhanced as David states so well in Psalm 27:4, *"One thing I have desired of the Lord, that will I seek: that I may dwell in the house of the Lord all the days of my life, to behold the beauty of the Lord, and to inquire in His temple."*

Usually, in the body of Christ, we can agree on worship and prayer. I have noticed the younger generation does not want to attend prayer meetings that are purely prayer; but there is an attraction of this generation to worship and prayer. As Psalm 133 states, the commanded blessing is on the heels of unity. United across the generations and denominations, the body of Christ is coming together in worship and prayer.

Worship added to prayer helps to keep us focused primarily on God. We agree with God and disagree with the enemy. We direct our worship and prayers primarily to God. There are two biblical categories of demonic spirits: those that dwell in people and those that dwell in heavenly places called principalities, powers, rulers of darkness of this age and spiritual hosts of wickedness (see Eph. 6:12). As a rule, we are to directly rebuke spirits that dwell inside humans. However, we dismantle principalities in the heavens by directly addressing God. In worship we war, in battle we soar!

In the place of persistent worship and prayer, we have ample opportunity to train others in the Word and in worship. "The singing seminary," the House of Prayer has been called. I have personally seen some of the most amazing worship leaders, musicians, singers, and intercessors raised up in the House of Prayer.

CONNECTION TO TODAY

If we return to Psalm 132 where David first vowed he would not go about ordinary life without a breakthrough in the Presence of God, he also said, *"Let us go into His tabernacle; let us worship at His footstool. Arise, O Lord, to Your resting place, You and the ark of Your strength. Let Your priests be clothed with righteousness, and let Your saints shout for joy"* (Ps. 132:7-9).

The Lord responds to David that He had chosen Zion (Jerusalem) for His dwelling place, a resting place and *"There I will make the horn of David grow; I will prepare a lamp for My Anointed"* (Ps. 132:13-17). "Horn" means government, and "Anointed" means Messiah. This is parallel to the Davidic Covenant the Lord makes with David in Second Samuel 7, where it is prophesied that David's rule will not end. The Anointed Messiah will come from the lineage of David to rule forever.

The tie of the Tabernacle of David to today is recorded in Amos: *"'On that day, I will raise up the Tabernacle of David, which has fallen down, and repair its damages. I will raise up its ruins, and rebuild it as in the days of old...Behold, the days are coming,' says the Lord, 'when the plowman shall overtake the reaper, and the treader of grapes him who sows seed'"* (Amos 9:11,13). This prophecy is repeated in Acts 15:15-17, which states, *"And the words of the prophets agree, just as it is written: 'After this I will return and will rebuild the tabernacle of*

David, which has fallen down; I will rebuild its ruins, and I will set it up; so that the rest of mankind may seek the Lord, even all the Gentiles who are called by My name, says the Lord who does all these things.'"

Resurgence of the Tabernacle

It is prophesied that in the last days there will be resurgence in the spirit, values, and principles of the Tabernacle of David. Night and day prayer and worship like David instituted will be raised up again. In 1984 there were 25 known 24/7 prayer ministries on the earth. Today, there is an estimated 20,000 such Houses of Prayer. It is not only the 24-hour-a-day houses of prayer that have impact on the earth. There are many centers of persistent prayer and worship around the globe operating at various amounts of hours per week. I have personally seen houses of prayer in the back of a truck, in a storefront facility, in the upper room of a bookstore, in one of the rooms of a doctor's office, in the midst of a red-light district, in a mountainous region, in a home in cottage country, in a church auditorium, and in a mall.

Being a House of Prayer leader, I work with a lot of next generation singers, musicians, and intercessors. In fact, I'm amazed at how this next generation is "hearing the sound of the Lord" to fast, pray and, worship unlike any other generation before. As the Lord spoke to me about starting Houses of Prayer, He said, "If you build it, they will come." And come they have. From Australia, Europe, Asia, Africa, from North and South America, the Lord has sent us young people giving themselves to persistent prayer and worship. I have witnessed firsthand their hearts become transformed, their passion for Jesus arise, their knowledge of the Word expand as they study, sing, and pray it.

How do you motivate a young person to spend hours a day in the place of prayer and worship? You can model it, teach it, impart it, pray for it. But the bottom line is, it is their heart meeting with God Himself. He shows up! His Presence is transforming! We should do what we can do, but we can't do what only God can do.

Indeed the words of Amos 9:11 are being fulfilled in our day. This resurgence of prayer and worship is helping to usher in two epic events. Firstly, a great harvest of souls into the Kingdom of God, the greatest revival the earth has ever seen. Secondly, the raising up of persistent prayer is part of the culmination of the age, and the second coming of Jesus. The Spirit and the Bride say to the Root and Offspring of David, the Bright and Morning Star, our Bridegroom, King, and Judge Jesus, *"Come!"* (see Rev. 22:16-17).

Prophecy

Chapter 7

WHY PROPHECY?

Pursue love, and desire spiritual gifts, but
especially that you may prophesy.
—1 CORINTHIANS 14:1

When the Lord admonishes us in First Corinthians 14:1 to desire spiritual gifts, especially that one may prophesy, He knows the great benefit this gift brings to our lives. The word "desire" in the Greek is *zeloo*, which means "to be zealous for, to burn with desire, to pursue ardently, to go after intensely."

Forty percent of the Bible is recorded prophecy or revelation. There are 300 prophecies in the Old Testament of Jesus' first coming, all of which came to pass. There are an estimated 150 different chapters and 2,400 different verses that prophesy of Jesus' second coming. They will all come to pass.

A prophetic awakening is happening in the body of Christ, and has been happening over the last few decades. Years ago, hearing of prophets or prophetically gifted people on the earth in modern times seemed like foreign language. That is not the case today as prophecy is embraced in more and more circles.

Looking at the world, there is great fascination with the supernatural. Hence the rise of psychics, mystics, palm readers, horoscopes, occult board games, and television shows and movies about the paranormal. What is happening? They are hungry for the supernatural. But these things are all just a forgery of the real thing: the church of Jesus Christ has the real deal on the supernatural. True believers have the Holy Spirit, access to heavenly places, revelation, and encounters with the supernatural. The problem is, many are not utilizing what has been made available for them through the shed blood of Jesus.

The prophesy of Acts 2:17-21, which directly quotes Joel 2, is even more true of this day than the day of its declaration. Peter gave this as part of his sermon at Pentecost, which was a partial fulfillment of these words. We are entering the days of the greater fulfillment or fuller expression of this word:

> *And it shall come to pass in the last days, says God, that I will pour out of My Spirit on all flesh; Your sons and your daughters shall prophesy, Your young men shall see visions, Your old men shall dream dreams. And on My menservants and on My maidservants I will pour out My Spirit in those days; and they shall prophesy. I will show wonders in Heaven above and signs in the earth beneath: Blood and fire and vapor of smoke. The sun shall be turned into darkness, and the moon into blood, before the coming of the great and awesome day of the*

Lord. And it shall come to pass that whoever calls on the name of the Lord shall be saved.

The Shepherd's Voice

There is an invitation given to us to live prophetic lives, under the leadership and in direct communion with our Commander-in-Chief. Jesus declared, *"My sheep hear My voice, and I know them, and they follow Me"* (John 10:27).

What a beautiful illustration Jesus used here. In biblical times, shepherds of different flocks would put their sheep into a common stone pen at night to protect them from devouring animals. In the morning, to take their sheep out to graze, the shepherds would call for their sheep to come and follow them. The sheep would know the voice of their particular shepherd and follow him out to the proper pasture. Similarly, we are called to hear the voice of our Shepherd with accuracy and walk in full obedience.

THE OFFICE OF A PROPHET VERSUS THE GIFT OF PROPHECY

The offices of apostles, prophets, evangelists, pastors and teachers are listed in Ephesians 4:11-13. The reason for the offices is *"for the equipping of the saints for the work of the ministry, for the edifying of the body of Christ, till we all come to the unity of the faith and of the knowledge of the Son of God"* (Eph. 4:12-13). Notice these offices are primarily about blessing and raising up others in the body of Christ.

The Office of a Prophet

The office of a prophet will usually signify someone who has a wider calling than a local church. Usually their reach of influence will be national or international.

First Corinthians 12:28 states, *"And God has appointed these in the church: first apostles, second prophets...."* There is a divine order in the body of Christ as it pertains to leadership. Biblically, we need all the gifts functioning together. Yet the apostle is to lead. Churches led by prophets tend to lack necessary care for individuals, may be more given to abrupt changes based on what the prophet may think the Lord is saying. Often these churches can lack stability.

The following can summarize the emphasis of each of the different offices: Apostles think big picture and are great visionaries and shapers. The prophets help bring clarity to what God is highlighting and saying; they tend to be very passionate for the heart of God. The pastor loves the people of the church and is big hearted by nature, wanting people to be cared for. The evangelist isn't so concerned about the people of the church but loves the lost and wants to mobilize all to "get outside of the walls of the church." The teacher loves the Word, and digs deep for meaning in it.

Those with an office of prophet will gravitate to Apostolic Centers as opposed to a ministry operating solely as a local church. In brief, Apostolic Centers are apostle led, kingdom focused, large in vision, equipping, training, and sending centers. Local churches that are pastor led are congregation focused and less inclined to equipping, training and sending. The prophet, along with the apostle, thinks big picture, is more inclined to hear from Heaven and want "Heaven on earth" at all cost.

There are scriptural examples of apostles working together with the prophets such as Paul and Silas. Silas is called a prophet, and he worked with the Apostle Paul exhorting and strengthening the churches (see Acts 15:32). Paul and the prophet Agabus also worked together (see Acts 21). Daniel was a prophet who worked under four kings, Nebuchadnezzar, Belshazzar, Darius and Cyrus. He was a voice of truth to each king. David had three prophets in his life:

the older prophet Samuel, his contemporary Nathan, and Gad the younger prophet. We need each other in the body of Christ and for all the gifts to function together in unity.

The Gift of Prophecy

The gift of prophecy, mentioned as one of the gifts in First Corinthians 12, is the one primarily explored in First Corinthians 14. It is a gift but is also something that can be developed. It is primarily for the edification, exhortation, and comfort of the body of Christ. First Corinthians 14:31 states that we can all prophesy. That would apply to the gift of prophecy, freely given by the Holy Spirit, through faith. However, not all will attain to an office of prophet but those whom the Father has anointed, appointed, and who respond to the call in obedience.

LIVING A PROPHETIC LIFESTYLE

The greatest reason to pursue a prophetic life is to foster an intimate, unified communion and fellowship with the Lord. Song of Solomon 5:6 declares, *"My heart leaped up when he spoke."* Indeed our hearts are awakened in love by the sound of His voice.

We receive encouragement and edification when we hear the voice of God, and we are to give these virtues to others when we give prophetic words (see 1 Cor. 14:3,12,26).

Comfort to our hearts and others is imparted through revelation. Isaiah 40:1 says, *"Comfort, yes, comfort My people!' says your God."* Getting God's perspective is very encouraging and consoling.

We receive divine direction for our lives as we press into the heart of God for His will and ways. When Peter had caught nothing when fishing all night, Jesus came and said, *"Launch out into the deep and let down your nets for a catch"* (Luke 5:4-5). Peter replied that at Jesus' word, he would obey. He then caught a huge haul of fish.

Psalm 119:105 states, *"Your word is a lamp unto my feet and a light unto my path."* Hearing the words of the Lord builds our faith and enables us to step out in obedience fearlessly. Romans 10:17 says, *"So faith comes by hearing, and hearing by the word of God."* An Old Testament example of the faith-building work of prophesy is recorded in Ezra 6:14 in relation to the rebuilding of the temple, *"So the elders of the Jews built, and they prospered through the prophesying of Haggai the prophet and Zechariah, the son of Iddo. And they built and finished it, according to the commandment of the God of Israel."*

Similar to building faith, living a prophetic lifestyle enables us to succeed or prosper in those things we put our hands to on which the Lord is breathing life. John 15:7-8 says, *"If you abide in Me, and My words abide in you, you will ask what you desire, and it shall be done for you. By this My Father is glorified, that you bear much fruit; so you will be My disciples."* Abiding in the words of God leads us to bear fruit. And Second Chronicles 20:20, said to be the verse of "20/20 vision" states, *"Believe in the Lord your God, and you shall be established; believe His prophets, and you shall prosper."*

Effects of a Prophetic Lifestyle

Living a prophetic lifestyle helps point us to a greater truth or a higher realm of reality. King Nebuchadnezzar said to Daniel, *"God is a revealer of secrets"* (Dan. 2:47). The spirit of prophecy is the testimony of Jesus (see Rev. 19:10). In the Greek, "testimony" is the word *marturia* meaning "witness or historical attestation." Another way of asking what this means is, "What does God say about that?" For example, if a doctor's report says one has an incurable illness and preparations need to be made to die, there is a need to get into the words of God and find out what He says about that. He is the final authority and source of truth.

As we will see more later, the prophetic gift can be used to bring the lost into salvation. First Corinthians 14:24-25 says, *"But if all prophesy, and an unbeliever or an uninformed person comes in, he is convinced by all, he is convicted by all. And thus the secrets of his heart are revealed; and so, falling down on his face, he will worship God and report that God is truly among you."*

The prophetic has been used constructively to bring correction and the conviction of the Holy Spirit to hearts. Nathan the prophet came to David after the Bathsheba incident, prompting David's repentance. Jeremiah came to King Zedekiah to prophesy the judgment of God, the impending fall of Jerusalem to Babylon, and implored him to surrender to the Babylonian King Nebuchadnezzar. King Zedekiah, unlike David, remained unrepentant and did not heed the word, and all that Jeremiah prophesied came to pass.

The Words of God

Jesus declared in John 6:63, *"It is the Spirit who gives life; the flesh profits nothing. The words that I speak to you are spirit, and they are life."* The words of God create life. How did the world come into existence? God spoke! When God speaks vision to us, we become "pregnant" by the spirit and we help bring His will into existence with our cooperation.

The words of God sustain life. Hebrews 1:3 says God is *upholding all things by the word of His power."* His word sustains life on earth, as we know it. His word sustains us. Some of the best prophetic words we can get are the ones that say something like, "Keep going. You are on the right track. Don't give up."

The word of God releases life. The words of God speak life to our heart, life to God-given dreams, and are originated and backed by the Spirit of God.

HEARING THE VOICE OF GOD

Technically speaking, Father God is in Heaven and Jesus is seated at His right hand (see Eph. 1:20; Heb. 8:1). The part of the Trinity with us here on earth, inhabiting or abiding within every true believer, is the Holy Spirit. He is our comforter, counselor, teacher, guide, leader, source of power, anointing, giver of gifts, and fruit bearer.

Additionally, part of the role of the Holy Spirit is to speak to us. Jesus states this in John 16:12-15: *"I still have many things to say to you, but you cannot bear them now. However, when He, the Spirit of truth, has come, He will guide you into all truth; for He will not speak on His own authority, but whatever He hears, He will speak; and He will tell you things to come. He will glorify Me, for He will take of what is Mine and declare it to you. All things that the Father has are Mine. Therefore I said that He will take of Mine and declare it to you."*

The Holy Spirit represents the Father and Son consistently. When we seek to "hear" from this supernatural realm, we do not listen outwardly but rather inwardly. The Hebrew word for prophet is *naba*, meaning to "bubble up." The prophetic words bubble up from the Spirit who tabernacles in our innermost being.

Mark Virkler's Four Keys

The teachings of Mark Virkler changed my life dramatically (see www.CWGMinistries.org). Mark, a former Baptist minister, took a year out of his life to learn how to hear the voice of God. That time of study brought him to four simple keys from Habakkuk 2:1-2: *"I will stand my watch and set myself on the rampart, and watch to see what He will say to me, and what I will answer when I am corrected. Then the Lord answered me and said: 'Write the vision....'*

Key #1: God's voice in your heart often sounds like a flow of spontaneous thoughts. Where we may be expecting God to speak to us in an audible voice or booming inner channel, more often He speaks in spontaneous thoughts, visions, feelings, or impressions.

Key #2: Become still, so you can sense God's flow of thoughts and emotions within. *"I will stand my watch* (on my guard post)...." Dialing down the busyness of our minds and our lives is helpful to tune into the sweet stillness of the Spirit's Presence.

Key #3: As you pray, fix the eyes of your heart upon Jesus. *"I will...watch to see what He will say to me...."* Turning our inner attention to the Lord, opening the eyes of our heart or understanding awakens the divine flow from within. Ephesians 1:18 speaks of the *"eyes of our understanding* [heart] *being enlightened."*

Key #4: Journaling, the writing out of your prayers and God's answers, brings great freedom in hearing God's voice. Habakkuk 2:2 says, *"Then the Lord answered me and said: 'Write* [record] *the vision....'"* Tapping into a flow of the spontaneous words and vision of God helps when it is recorded. Testing the words later to ensure that they align with scripture and the character and nature of God are necessary.

Test the Words You Hear

Bill Johnson, senior leader of Bethel Church in Redding, California said, "Learning to discern the voice of the Lord and the voice of the accuser is imperative to dispelling confusion."[35] We can hear what others say and what our culture says, but when we get into the Presence of God and hear what He has to say, all confusion leaves, peace pervades, and we know the will of God.

John Arnott, founding leader of Catch the Fire Ministries and a spiritual father to me, has said many times, "We need to trust the Lord's ability to lead us more than the enemy's ability to deceive us." When learning to hear the voice of God, we will make mistakes. To hear God is both a gift and something we develop. Similar to a child learning to walk who will fall down many times but will get back up again only to soon be running with confidence, we need to go through growth steps, refusing the temptation to quit. We also need to be humble and teachable in the prophetic, repenting if we spoke a word wrongly, being open to correction and willing to admit if we are wrong.

Ways to Test What You Hear

Scripture teaches us to judge the prophetic (see 1 Cor. 14:29). Whatever is of the Lord will pass His tests. Here are some tests to determine if what is received by revelation is indeed from God or not.

1. Whatever we believe is of the Lord will be consistent with the *logos*, the written scriptures, of God.

2. It will be according to the love nature of the Lord since God is love (see 1 John 4:8).

3. Since it is the Holy Spirit who speaks to us, His words will be filled with the fruit of the Spirit: Love, joy, peace, patience, kindness, goodness, faithfulness, gentleness, and self-control (see Gal. 5:22-23). Anything we hear that makes us nervous, anxious, or lacking peace can be judged as not from the Spirit of God.

4. All true words from the Lord will be consistent with the testimony of Jesus (His witness, His words) as Revelation 19:10 declares.

5. The words of the Lord will be confirmed through others who hear His voice. Directional words should be acted upon only if there is sufficient confirmation.

6. Words can be judged by whether or not they come to pass. One gains a proven track record in the prophetic if words they have spoken come to pass. John and I do not allow just anyone to prophesy from the stage of the church we pastor. We do allow those who we know have both the character and proven track record to prophesy with our blessing.

7. The Father's words will also be in some way edifying, exhorting and comforting as First Corinthians 14:3 admonishes. Even when we are corrected or confronted to come higher in character and deeds, it will give us hope and take us ultimately to a place of edification.

8. Another test, which sounds simplistic but has much truth: everything negative is from the enemy and everything positive is from God. Even when God is convicting us or correcting us, He is still positive and life giving in His approach.

RHEMA WORDS

Confronted by satan with temptations, Jesus replied with authority, *"It is written, 'Man shall not live by bread alone, but by every word that proceeds from the mouth of God'"* (Matt. 4:4). In this passage, "word" comes from the Greek *rhema*, the spoken, uttered word of God. Hearing the voice of God is to be our daily bread, a regular partaking of food for our spirit. Just as proper nutrition sustains our physical bodies and is necessary for growth and health, so is hearing the voice of our Lord necessary for spiritual growth and health.

Not partaking of this spiritual sustenance of *rhema* grounded in the *logos* word of God can open us up to disease of religious spirits, placid spiritual existence, or worse yet, lukewarm, intellectually based affections for the Lord. Just as we need to sit down to eat our food each day and take the effort to prepare a meal and chew, swallow, and digest, so we also need to take the time to listen, position ourselves to hear the voice of the Lord, and make it a daily part of our spiritual journey.

His Thoughts Toward Us

Psalm 40:5 states, *"Your thoughts toward us cannot be recounted to You in order; if I would declare and speak of them, they are more than can be numbered."* Similarly, Psalm 139:17-18 says, *"How precious also are Your thoughts to me, O God! How great is the sum of them! If I should count them, they would be more in number than the sand."* God's thoughts toward us are more numerous than the grains of sand on the seashore. That is astounding!

Many times, I have walked a beach and thought of this passage. Imagine a desert and how much sand is in it. One handful alone of sand is said to contain approximately 10,000 grains. Yet God's thoughts toward you outnumber the sand. When we endeavor to hear His voice, we simply tap into those thoughts. There is never a shortage of His thoughts toward you. We never have to convince God to speak to us. He is an extremely communicative Father. Jeremiah 29:11-13 tells us the nature of these thoughts. *"For I know the thoughts that I think toward you, says the Lord, thoughts of peace and not of evil, to give you a future and a hope. Then you will call upon Me and go and pray to Me, and I will listen to you. And you will seek Me and find Me, when you search for Me with all your heart."*

Competing Voices

There are competitive voices that vie for our attention in the continuous inner dialogue within our soul and spirit. If we pay attention to this inner communication, we can often find negative thoughts about various topics like the weather, how we are feeling, how someone looks, how we have been unjustly treated, and on and on. When we began to pay attention to what is swirling around in our minds throughout the day, we may not impressed by what we find. The concept of "putting on the mind of Christ" needs to be practiced regularly until it becomes normalcy.

Years ago, I needed to war daily against the mental bombardment from the soulish, carnal nature, and from demonically inspired whispers. They sounded much like hopelessness, defeat, and reminders of where I didn't measure up. *"Casting down arguments and every high thing that exalts itself against the knowledge of God, bringing every thought into captivity to the obedience of Christ"* (2 Cor. 10:5) was not going to be an immediate quick fix. Years of negative thought patterns needed to be consistently surrendered to the Father by an act of my will as well as a divine work of His grace. Replacing negative thoughts can be as simple as purposely replacing them with positive ones.

Bill Johnson states, "The first reason for revelation is to transform us."[36] Life-altering revelation awaits us as we take the time to position ourselves in faith to hear the voice of God. My life has radically been altered due to regular hearing and recording the words of life spoken to me by my loving heavenly Father.

Strongholds in Our Mind

Remember, *"the weapons of our warfare are not carnal but mighty in God for pulling down strongholds"* (2 Cor. 10:4). The strongholds in our mind will come down by the power of the Lord in partnership with our willingness and desire for change. The mind is indeed a battlefield, and what better way to win that battle then to dwell consistently on the numerous thoughts of our heavenly Father coming to us which are full of life, victory, and love.

Romans 12:2 states, *"And do not be conformed to this world, but be transformed by the renewing of your mind, that you may prove what is that good and acceptable and perfect will of God."* Transformation in our minds, mouths, actions, behaviors, and habits are all linked.

Ephesians 4:22-24 gives the key to death to the old and life to the new: *"That you put off, concerning your former conduct, the old man which grows corrupt according to the deceitful lusts, and be renewed in the spirit of your mind, and that you put on the new man which was created according to God, in true righteousness and holiness."* Notice the "bridge to cross," leaving the old you behind and living to the new you: It is *"be renewed in the spirit of your mind."*

The spoken word of God into our spirits causes our faith to arise for what He says to us. His destiny, His plan, and His way revealed may contradict our limited, finite thinking; but dwelling long enough on His words will lift our eyes to see from a heavenly perspective.

Believing a Lie

My husband John believed a lie for years that went along these lines: "I can't really hear God. That is not my gift. I am more logical and rational." It is true John is wise and I call him a "walking concordance," since if I ask him where a particular scripture is located in the Bible, he will immediately know the reference. Yet that lie he believed kept him from hearing the still, small voice of God. A visiting prophetic person called John out of a crowd of people one day and said, "Sir, you need to stop leaning on your wife's ability to hear God. You can hear God for yourself."

Well, you might have thought I'd paid that discerning man to say that over my husband since I'd been admonishing him to practice hearing God's voice. When John repented of believing the lie that he could not hear God, it was as if a ceiling lifted off of him or some unseen cotton in his spiritual ears was removed as he then began to hear God clearly and regularly since that time. Repentance may be needed if one has believed that lie, or any lie for that matter. I have said many times, "Heaven and hell are both looking for human agreement. Who are you going to agree with?"

In Hebrews chapter 5, the writer admonishes the reader to stop being immature, still dwelling on *"milk and not solid food"* for "solid food" is for those who are mature. Why this condition of immaturity? The writer gives us the answer in verse 11: *"Since you have become dull of hearing."* And the admonition is to exercise the revelatory to help us grow up (see Heb. 5:144).

Write It Down!

Recording the words God speaks to us is helpful in numerous ways. Otherwise so easily forgotten, one can look back and dwell on what God has spoken yesterday, last month, or even years ago. Recording helps us to test the words in the times to come. We honor

His words as we record them, not allowing them to be dropped or considered as meaningless. Regular listening and recording the Lord's words to us helps us grow in the gift of prophecy. Exercising means growth, and our level of accuracy and proven track record increases as we regularly cultivate intimacy in hearing the voice of our beloved One.

What I have found most helpful is to journal every day, often starting early in the morning by writing the open-ended question: "What do You want to say to me today, Father?" I position myself quietly to hear with pen and paper in hand and simply record what I hear. Once finished, I may ask more specific questions about the day, things that may be concerning me, and other things I need to know from my Heavenly Father. Then, when I'm going about my day, the "tap" is still on to dialogue with the Lord as I walk, drive, or do whatever I'm doing. I don't write out all those dialogues but may record pertinent tidbits later. Journaling is not the only way to tap into the flow of the words of God. However, regular use will help us in hearing at any time and cause a flow of the prophetic to bubble up whenever needed.

The Prophetic Brings Increase

Proverbs 14:4 is a quirky proverb, which could have multiple levels of interpretation. It can apply to hearing God's voice and living a prophetic life: *"Where no oxen are, the trough is clean; but much increase comes by the strength of an ox."* When the prophetic is in your life, there is a bit of a mess to clean up at times. As mentioned, you may make mistakes in the process of growth. You also need to "feed" the gift, as in exercise and utilize it. However, learning to flow in hearing the voice of God helps bring the increase.

My husband and I rely heavily on hearing the voice of God for parenting. We know we have a perfect Father in Heaven who knows best how to parent our children. Regular petitions for His wisdom in this area have yielded wonderful results in six children who passionately love the Lord and are growing in His destiny for them.

Hearing the voice of the Lord for insights into your workplace, to help take right steps in your relationships, and for any minor or major decision will all help usher in supernatural assistance. Similarly, in the sense of leadership of a church or ministry, when you have the prophetic in the "house," you have the strength of increase it brings. You also need to pastor the prophetic and those who particularly flow in the gift.

Receive Healing for Bad Experiences

First Thessalonians 5:19-20 puts it well: *"Do not quench the Sprit. Do not despise prophecies."* This counsel is important personally as well as corporately in ministry. Do not "throw the baby out with the bathwater" if there have been negative prophetic experiences in your life or ministry. Pastor it, get healed where healing is needed, forgive, and get onto embracing the prophetic and the myriads of benefits of living a prophetic life and having a prophetic church.

I heard a story from a friend who was with a former International Christian leader some months before this Christian leader died of an incurable illness. The man dealing with the sickness spoke of regrets as a leader, saying he could no longer hear the voice of God. He admitted that he had removed the practice of prophecy from his church. The clamor of the other voices—including that of his circle of leaders—had been louder to him than the voice of God. Now, in his older age and facing a soon departure from earth, he was filled with regrets that he hadn't cultivated more of that close relationship with the living God rather than being so busy in meetings, getting human advice, or doing the "work" of the ministry.

One thing we will never regret as we approach that day when we leave this earth: the time, energy, money, and commitment we make to seek the face of Jesus day after day after day.

"What Do You Want to Say?"

Take the time to position yourself right now to hear the voice of the One who loves to communicate with you. Dial down the busyness of your mind, tune into the spontaneous flow of thoughts that come to you, fix your eyes on Jesus, and simply ask, "What do you want to say to me?" Record what you hear, even if it starts with one word or phrase. From there, allow the words to flow. His thoughts toward you are flowing, as numerous as the sand. Receive them.

Next, we will see how the prophetic brings transformation to us and through us to the world around us.

Chapter 8

REVELATION

There are basically three aspects to prophesy. Revelation, meaning what we get from God; interpretation, the meaning of the revelation; and application, what do we do with the revelation?

HOW DOES GOD SPEAK?

There are various ways that the Lord may choose to speak to us by way of revelation. We will examine some here:

The Word of God—The most important way we hear God is through His Word. As discussed earlier, the scriptures are the ultimate plumb line by which we measure other revelation. The Holy scriptures are able to make us wise (see 2 Tim. 3:15).

Still, small voice of God—Elijah did not hear God in the wind, earthquake, or fire, but only in the still, small voice (see 1 Kings 19:11-13). Often, the still, small voice sounds like our own thoughts as the Lord communicates to us subtly as His thoughts invade ours (see Ps. 40:5).

Visions / Pictures—We can see in the spirit through still pictures or unfolding visions as the eyes of our understanding are enlightened by the Holy Spirit. (More on this is in the section entitled, "The Seeing Realm.")

Dreams—Dreams are an important way God speaks to His people. (See more on dreams in the coming section entitled, "Dreams.")

Things in the Natural that speak of the supernatural—God can speak spiritual messages through nature. Psalm 19:1 says, *"The heavens declare the glory of God; and the firmament shows His handiwork."* How can one deny the existence of God when you see the multitudes of stars, the complexity of human anatomy, or the beauty of a sunset? Additionally, the Lord can use seemingly ordinary things to speak to us: a newspaper heading, a billboard, or a particular object that crosses our path at a specific moment in time.

John and I were once driving on country roads while discussing our children's department in the church we pastored at the time. We realized the department needed help and we were discussing if we should take turns leading kids ministry or what should be done. At that moment we came upon a car in front of us with the license plate ACTZ 636. Immediately we said to one another, "Acts 6:3-6! I wonder what that says." I got out my Bible to read how the apostles were faced with a need for practical help in the ministry. They decided it wise to seek out others to lead this department and they said, *"But we will give ourselves continually to prayer and the ministry of the word"* (Acts 6:4). It goes on to say how they chose Stephen and six others and laid hands on them to commission them. Amazingly, it was a couple months after this incident where the Lord gave us a man named Stephen to lead our children's ministry.

Word of Wisdom—When the Lord gives divine instruction, blueprints, or insight into certain situations, it can be called a word of wisdom (see 1 Cor. 12:8). As we ask for wisdom in life circumstances, we will receive it.

Word of Knowledge—A word of knowledge is simply insight or information given divinely (see 1 Cor. 12:8). This is particularly helpful in prophetic evangelism, where information divinely received about an individual often helps open their hearts to the revelation that there is indeed a God who knows all things about them (see 1 Cor. 14:24-25).

Discernment—Also referred to as impressions, discernment is the ability to differentiate what is of God and what is not (see 1 Cor. 12:10; 1 John 4:1). We can receive from the Holy Spirit discernment of gifts, spirits, actions, intentions, and discernment of the times we are living in (see Matt. 16:2-3). Especially as the evil one parades himself as an angel of light, discernment is needed to not participate in things not pleasing to the Lord. I have found that my discernment for which movies are okay for my children to watch and which are not okay has grown over the years. A check in my spirit will indicate what movie or music is not acceptable, often from just hearing its title or looking at an ad for it. We need to pay attention to our impressions (gut instinct) as we become more and more holy, given to the Lord, and sanctified, our impressions and discernment will increase in accuracy.

Years ago we started to experience money disappearing from our home. Our son was missing $400 from his room from the sale of his dog. Money was missing from drawers and wallets. It was troubling. After interviewing our children and the helper who lived with us, we knew no one in our home was stealing the money. We had next-door neighbors who outwardly appeared to have it all together. They were a good-looking family of four with a son and daughter who were friends with our kids. Their house was larger than ours; they drove fancy, new cars, and dressed impeccably. However, my discernment rose up and somehow I knew the wife in this family was the one taking the money from us. We had no proof initially but our helper had befriended this woman and sought to witness to her, having her over for tea when we were not at home. Sure enough, we did catch her stealing from us and it came to light that this woman was a kleptomaniac: someone who compulsively steals, not necessarily for personal gain but because an inner urge to steal is so powerful. Listen to the discernment God is giving you all the while not giving into unrighteous judgments. True discernment will be proven with time.

Peace or Lack of Peace—Since peace is one of the fruit of the Spirit (see Gal. 5:22) the Spirit will use peace as a way to communicate to us. Particularly for decisions that need to be made; do you have peace with a decision or path of action, or lack of peace? John and I have found a great safety in ensuring both of us have peace before proceeding in important decisions that affect our family. If one or the other of us does not have peace, we will not go forward. We have seen this save us from trouble time and again.

Circumstances—Doors that open and doors that close can be indications of God's will. If we are banging on doors that simply refuse to budge, it isn't always the devil holding it closed. It may not be the best for you or the timing may not be right. When the disciples would come to a city that refused them, they were instructed to shake the dust off their feet and go elsewhere (see Matt. 10:14). When Paul found himself shipwrecked on the island of Malta, it only opened up an opportunity to bring the gospel of salvation and healing to that land (see Acts 28).

Others—The Lord certainly uses other people to speak to us. They may be giving us a prophecy (see 1 Cor. 14), or they may simply be telling a story, or speaking to us in a casual setting but something they say resonates within us as being a word from the Lord. Preachers and teachers certainly communicate to us from the Lord. Sometimes we can receive words from less likely sources such as little children. When our daughter Zoe was six years old, she scribbled a note to my husband, "Dad I want you to come home." It struck him powerfully that he was too busy and needed to prioritize his time to be home more with the family.

Angels—Biblical precedence for angelic activity is large in scope and amount. Angels are used to deliver messages (see Dan. 9:21-22), war with the demonic (see Dan. 10:13), protect (see Ps. 91:11-12), bring freedom (see Acts 5:19), minister to God's people (see Heb. 1:14), worship the Lord and do His bidding (see Ps. 103:20-21). When I was eight years old, two individuals came to my family's farm and spoke to me. They told me of things to come in my life, many of which have already been fulfilled. They also spoke of a great harvest of souls I would see in my lifetime. I never forgot the interaction as it branded me for the rest of my life to want to know and serve the Lord. When I asked my mother, working nearby, whom the people were who came to speak with me, she replied, "What people?" Later I would read in Hebrews 13:2 how angels can appear in human form.

Audible Voice of God—The Lord spoke audibly throughout the Bible. A significant interaction occurred at Jesus' baptism where the Father affirmed His Son, *"You are My beloved Son; in You I am well pleased"* (Luke 3:22). My grandmother had been in great pain with arthritis for years. One day, she was praying on her knees for others as she did every day, when she heard the audible, booming voice of God say, "Pray for yourself." She was stunned, and used to praying for everyone else; it took the same message to come three times before my grandmother did pray for herself and she was instantly healed of all arthritis for the rest of her life.

INTERPRETATION

When the butler and the baker of the king of Egypt were in the same prison as Joseph, they were troubled by the fact that they had dreams but there was no one to interpret them. Joseph said to them, *"Do not interpretations belong to God?"* (Gen. 40:8). Similarly, when King Nebuchadnezzar demanded not only the interpretation but also his dream to be revealed, Daniel 2:27-28 tells us, *"Daniel answered in the presence of the king, and said, 'The secret which the king has demanded, the wise men, the astrologers, the magicians, and the soothsayers cannot declare to the king. But there is a God in Heaven who reveals secrets, and He has made known to King Nebuchadnezzar what will be in the latter days.'"*

Symbolism in Dreams

Interpretation of dreams, visions, and prophetic revelation comes from God. I do not agree with the reduction of interpretation of dreams or visions based on symbolism alone. That is what the psychics do. To interpret solely based on symbols is not healthy.

However, neither should we completely dismiss all symbolism. There will be times when certain objects or people remind us of related themes. Often this will be of meaning to you as an individual. A former teacher in your dream will mean something to you, whereas that person may not mean anything to another. A dog to one may mean a friend whereas to another it may invoke fear or dislike. In other words, there may be some truth to symbols holding certain meanings in prophetic revelation.

It has been said vehicles can symbolize "ministry." For example, a car may mean someone's individual ministry, a bigger vehicle such as a bus can mean a church ministry, or an airplane can mean international ministry. One day, a young man from our church who was the drummer on the worship team, came to me and said he had a dream that he was driving a bus filled with young people. Immediately the Lord gave me the interpretation that he was going to become a young pastor in a church. That indeed came to pass three months later when he was asked to move to Australia to become a youth pastor at a church.

The more we grow in Him, the more clear revelation becomes. I have also noticed in the many years that I have spent training prophetic people, the more you grow in the Lord, the more you will have literal dreams. Additionally, often if you are an active participant in your dream, it may be more likely a dream meant for you. If you are a mere observer in your dream, it can hold a broader interpretation.

There can be interpretation pitfalls such as having an idol in our hearts. If we greatly desire something, we may "hear" God saying we are going to get it when all along it is actually our will imposing a skewed interpretation. Additionally, unhealed hurts in our hearts, unforgiveness, willful ongoing sin in one's life, or a lack of revelation of the Father's love can all lead to misled interpretations. I have also noticed that sometimes prophetic people can pick up on someone's desires and begin to prophesy into that desire. It is important to not prophecy into someone's desires but God's desires. We grow in discerning accurate interpretation to what we receive in revelation.

APPLICATION

Amos 3:7 says, *"Surely the Lord God does nothing, unless He reveals His secret to His servants the prophets."* Many times the Lord wants to reveal His secrets to us because we are close to Him. Who do you reveal your secrets to? Someone you barely know? We reveal intimate details to those we are well acquainted with and to those whom we trust. The Lord wants to reveal secrets to us. Sometimes He shares them for us to proclaim, other times to pray into and at other times, just because He wants fellowship. So much of living a prophetic life means we receive revelation from the Lord that was never meant to be shared on earth. I once heard a prophetic man say, "Prophets are known on earth for what they say, but they are known in Heaven for what they don't say."

It has been said, "Prophesy is the springboard into the pool of prayer." The prophetic call and the intercessory call go hand in hand. The biblical prophets were also intercessors! Jeremiah 27:18 says, *"But if they are prophets, and if the word of the Lord is with them, let them now make intercession to the Lord of hosts."*

Negative revelations (warning revelation or insights into what the enemy is up to) are to be first bathed in prayer before they are shared. If an individual is constantly receiving negative revelation, there may be a pattern of belief in that individual of how big the enemy is, as opposed to the truth of "great big God, itty, bitty devil."

I have both been a prophetic voice in churches as well as a pastor (and still am) and I can say firsthand that pastors don't necessarily want to hear all the dark, warning revelation. In fact, it has served to alienate some pastors from the prophetic, intercessory types when all they hear is negative revelation. We need a clear grip on how big God is as well as how our prayers are effective in thwarting the plans of darkness.

Practically speaking, application of prophetic words in a corporate setting should involve submission of the word to whoever is in charge of the meeting, prior to giving it. It may be a pastor or meeting host who needs to hear what the Lord is showing you before you are released to share publicly. When someone stands up from the back of an auditorium and shouts out a word, it is not in line with God's order of honoring leadership and the ones entrusted to shepherding those sheep. Additionally, there are appropriate times given to share corporate prophetic words. If one has battled in knowing if their word is from God or themselves and suddenly decides it is from God but the worship and announcement time is over and the speaker has begun, the timing has simply passed. Words can be written out and handed to leadership, which can be judged and viewed later.

First Corinthians 13:2 states, *"And though I have the gift of prophecy, and understand all mysteries and all knowledge, and though I have all faith, so that I could remove mountains, but have not love, I am nothing."* In application of prophecy, it is vital to be one who lives to love. Prophecy without love for the Lord or love for His Bride can be a dangerous, destructive weapon. Prophetic insight into the sins of individuals called out publicly has led to humiliation and dislike or even outright rejection of the gift. Prophecy bathed in love is a precious tool able to bring many into close fellowship with their Creator. If one does not love the Bride of Christ, one should not attain to prophesy.

However, with a heart filled with love, it is good to practice prophecy. Use the gift in opportunities that arise for you in small groups, with other believers as well as out on the streets with those who need to know the love of God.

Chapter 9

THE SEEING REALM

*L*et us turn to aspects of vision and the seeing realm. In response to the lukewarm condition of the Laodicean church, the Lord admonishes them to *"anoint your eyes with eye salve, that you may see"* (Rev. 3:18). When we see in the Spirit it plugs us into God's limitless greatness.

Ephesians 1:17-18 states, *"That the God of our Lord Jesus Christ, the Father of glory, may give to you the spirit of wisdom and revelation in the knowledge of Him, the eyes of your understanding being enlightened; that you may know what is the hope of His calling, what are the riches of the glory of His inheritance in the saints."* The eyes of our understanding can be opened by the power of the Holy Spirit. We may have visions or prophetic pictures come to us as we ask for them and position ourselves to receive, or they may come simply as we are going through life. Jesus only did those things He saw His

Father doing (see John 5:19). We too, like Jesus, can see what the Father wants to do through us and act in kind.

PICTURES AND VISIONS

We will now examine how one can see with spiritual senses, with the eyes of our hearts, messages that may come as pictures or visions. At times, the Lord will highlight ordinary objects to speak spiritual truths to us.

What the Prophets in the Bible Saw

The Lord asked the prophet Jeremiah what he saw, to which Jeremiah replied, *"I see a branch of an almond tree"* (Jer. 1:11). The Lord then replied, *"You have seen well, for I am ready (watching) to perform My word"* (Jer. 1:12). In Hebrew, the words "almond" and "watching" sound very similar. The almond tree blooms early in the spring, becoming the tree that is ready and watching as all the other blossoms unfold. Through Jeremiah's vision of the branch of an almond tree, the Lord speaks about the fact that He will watch over His word to bring about His promises.

An angel similarly asks the prophet Zechariah what he saw, to which he responded that he saw a lampstand, a bowl, and two olive trees. Asking for the interpretation, Zechariah is given a prophetic word for Zerubbabel, who is attempting to rebuild the temple in Jerusalem. He is told, *"'Not by might nor by power, but by My Spirit,' says the Lord of hosts"* (Zech. 4:6).

Daniel received in a night vision the image King Nebuchadnezzar saw in a dream: The gold head, chest, and arms of silver, belly and thighs of bronze, legs of iron and feet of clay and iron, mixed. The Lord gives the interpretation to Daniel of the succession of kingdoms of Babylon, Medo-Persia, Greece, Rome, and a future revived Roman Empire. All will be crushed by the Kingdom of God, which will stand forever (see Dan. 2).

The prophet Agabus saw Paul being taken captive and bound by the Jews if he went to Jerusalem, dramatically acting out the picture or vision he saw of Paul's hands and feet being bound (see Acts 21:10-11). This did indeed happen not long after, although it was the Romans who bound Paul and not the Jews as Agabus thought. This is a good example of an accurate word with some inaccurate details.

Hearing or Seeing

I have found the still, small, voice of God familiar and easy to hear. Visions and pictures were common for me as a child but sadly mostly of the dark side as in seeing demons and things that frightened me. In a sense, I tried to turn off the ability to see. Thus, as an adult, I cried out to the Lord to forgive me for trying to turn off the ability to see and asked Him to reactivate the seer within me, but to see those things He was doing and what He wanted me to see.

For a period time, I actually sought to not lean only on the "hearing," but I began to develop the "seeing." A doctor will recommend the covering up of a good eye in the case of one weak or wandering eye. In other words, hold back on the good to develop the weak. As I sought to soak in God's Presence to see in the spirit, I found it developed more in my life.

We can "soak to see." Sometimes what we see may be very life altering and impactful. Other times, it may be a simple message. As you ask and practice, you will begin to see pictures and visions, and it is best to ask God for the interpretation of such pictures and visions. However, sometimes we give a picture to someone, not knowing the interpretation ourselves; but it may make perfect sense to that person.

DREAMS

Dreams, or night visions, are ways in which the Lord gives messages to His people.

Warning Dreams

The Lord appeared to Joseph four times around the time of Jesus' birth, all in warning dreams (see Matt. 1:20; 2:13,19-20,22).

On April 14, 1865, President Abraham Lincoln shared a dream he had with a small group including his wife and a trusted friend and former law partner, Ward Hill Lamon. Lamon later wrote about the contents of the dream. Lincoln "walked into the East Room of the White House to find a covered corpse guarded by soldiers and surrounded by a crowd of mourners. When Lincoln asked one of the soldiers who had died, the soldier replied, 'The president. He was killed by an assassin.'"[37] Lincoln told Lamon the dream "strangely annoyed" him ever since. Ten days after having the dream, Lincoln was shot dead by an assassin.[38]

The sinking of the Titanic in 1912 on its maiden voyage was an epic disaster in history, causing the death of 1,514 people. After the sinking, hundreds of people reported they had dreams or premonitions of the ship's demise. Nineteen of those are authenticated as they were documented or relayed to a second party prior to the sailing. Some of those with dreams cancelled their tickets onboard the ocean liner.

Survivor Eva Hart, who was seven years old at the time of the sinking, later claimed that her mother sat up every night rather than go to sleep on the Titanic because she was afraid there would be an accident. Her mother's quick action when feeling a "bump" in the night caused Eva and her mother to be saved as they were among the first to get on a lifeboat.[39]

Major Archibald Willingham Butt was traveling first-class on the ship and had a premonition he would not return home. He contacted his lawyer to arrange his last will and testament and closed up his affairs preparing for death. Major Butt perished in the sinking. Survivor Anne Ward, told her mother she did not want to make another voyage across the ocean as she had a premonition that something was going to happen to the ship on the maiden voyage.[40]

Creative Dreams

There have been various historical discoveries relayed in dreams. Considered the father of quantum mechanics, Niels Bohr, had an inspirational dream that led to his discovery of the structure of the atom. Albert Einstein came to the extraordinary scientific achievement of discovering the principle of relativity after having a vivid dream. Otto Loewi, a Nobel Prize winning pharmacologist discovered acetylcholine, responsible for the transmission of nerve impulses, in a dream repeated to him twice in consecutive nights. Frederick Banting, the Nobel Prize winner for the discovery of insulin as a drug to treat diabetes, got the revelation in two dreams. His discovery has saved or transformed the lives of millions of people.[41]

The Lord appeared to King Solomon in a dream saying, *"Ask! What shall I give you?"* (1 Kings 3:5). Remarkably, Solomon answers the Lord in the dream (see 1 Kings 3:6-9).

Gideon was greatly encouraged to go to battle against the Midianites and Amalekites after overhearing a dream of a Midianite, who dreamed that Gideon and his army would defeat them.

Sources of Dreams

However, not all dreams are from the Lord. There can be three sources of dreams:

Self Dreams—This is where the dream originates from one-self. The body may be communicating stress or distress or simply processing information. Sometimes watching a movie can cause disturbing dreams.

Dreams from the Enemy—These can be dreams that translate lies to us or harass us. Nightmares can be from an unhealed heart where a response is needed to bring healing into an area of wounding, or can also be where the enemy has somehow had access into a person's home or life. Nightmares can be used of the enemy to shut down the prophetic.

God Dreams—God dreams speak truth to our hearts, breaking through the paradigm of our thinking and showing us things about our hearts or lives we may not have been open to. They tend to be vivid, and they seem to stick with us.

Honor Your Dreams

Our tendency to dream heavenly dreams will increase as we honor our dreams. This can include writing them out, praying into them, paying attention to your dreams, dialoguing with God about them, and obeying instructions given in them.

Sarah Jackson, a leader in the Catch the Fire School Toronto of Ministry, is an avid dreamer and anointed dream interpreter. She teaches two questions to ask about the dream you have had:

- What am I supposed to receive or take away from this dream?
- Why did I have the dream now?

Sarah teaches that we need to look at where we are within the dream. If we are participating in the action or events of the dream, it is often for us and about us. If we are watching events as an observer but not participating, it may be for someone else, or of a corporate nature outside of ourselves.

We can also, at times, get too caught up in the details of the dream and trying to find meaning in them as opposed to simply getting the main point. Sarah teaches to summarize your dream in a sentence and even entitle your dream. Additionally, ask pertinent questions about the dream as you seek its meaning. Questions such as, "Why is it a car and not a bicycle? What does that animal in my dream mean to me? What is the meaning of the name of that person in my dream?"

What Do I Do with Dreams?

I have often experienced warnings in dreams, for the purpose of intercession against the strategies of evil. I've taught my children to look for the same. One morning our daughter Aquila awakened to a dream that our other daughter Phoebe fell and was badly injured. As I was preparing breakfast, Aquila and I prayed against the dream, asked God to protect Phoebe, and thwart any plans of evil. That afternoon I put Phoebe up for a nap in her third-story bedroom. The window was open but the window screen was in place. Phoebe began to play with the screen and somehow it was removed from its place. I heard my neighbor scream to me and I ran up to Phoebe's bedroom to pull her in from the window just as she was about to fall. This all happened hours after Aquila's dream. What if we hadn't stopped to pray? Don't assume negative dreams will come to pass; pray into them.

I've also received many directional dreams, which have helped steer the course of my life. We can ask the Lord for dreams in general and also for specific revelation we may need. When my husband John and I were praying about John leaving his job as a bank manager to go on staff at what was then called Toronto Airport

Christian Fellowship, I felt right away it was of the Lord. John needed to hear for himself, as it was risky to leave his stable job at the bank. The Lord gave him a dream. In the dream, John Arnott, the founding pastor at the Toronto church, came to John and said, "Come, come to Toronto with us." It was like the night vision Paul received recorded in Acts 16, when a man from Macedonia pleaded with Paul to come to Macedonia and help them. Paul immediately went to Macedonia after the dream. We immediately made preparations to move to Toronto after John's dream.

If you pay attention to your dreams, write them out, pray into them and honor them, you will receive more. Take the time to ask God to awaken your dream life and reveal mysteries to you in the night.

Chapter 10

SEEING IN THE SPIRIT REALM

The prophet Elisha was a menace to the Syrian army. He would receive revelation of their battle strategies and let the king of Israel know, eliminating the element of surprise for the enemy army. Hence, the Syrian king sent a large contingent of soldiers to surround the city and capture Elisha. When Elisha's servant saw the enemy army he was very concerned. Yet Elisha was not worried, told his servant not to fear, and prayed that the Lord would open his eyes into the spirit realm. When the servant's spiritual eyes were opened, he saw the mountain full of horses and chariots of fire all around Elisha. Elisha prayed again and the Lord struck the Syrian army with blindness; Elisha led that blind army straight to the king of Israel (see 2 Kings 6:11-23).

Elisha's ability to see in the spirit realm caused him to not fear what he saw in the natural. Indeed there is a very real realm of the angels and demons that perhaps can be considered more real than this "First Heaven" realm around us, where we see only with our natural eyesight. The supernatural realm, of which the angels are a part, is all around us, not limited to our natural realm. Satan was a created being that aspired to be God (see Ezek. 28) and was thus cast out of Heaven, taking one-third of the angels with him (see Rev. 12:4). These beings we now commonly refer to as demons. The good news is we have two thirds with us: the angels.

ANGELS

God dictates the work of angels. Psalm 103:20-21 says, *"Bless the Lord, you His angels, who excel in strength, who do His word, heeding the voice of His word. Bless the Lord, all you His hosts, you ministers of His, who do His pleasure."* And Psalm 104:4 says, *"Who makes His angels spirits, His ministers a flame of fire."*

There are numerous biblical references to the work of angels. An angel instructed Hagar to name her child Ishmael. Abraham had a discussion with the angels as to how many righteous men will save a city. Jacob dreamed of a ladder going into Heaven with the angels ascending and descending. The Angel of the Lord was sent before the children of Israel as they fled Egypt. An angel first appeared to Balaam's donkey and then to Balaam. Angels announced upcoming births to the parents of Isaac, Samson, John, and Jesus. An angel ministered to Elijah when he was tired, hungry, and depressed after running from Jezebel. An angel executed a plague on the Israelites as punishment for David taking the census. Seventy thousand of them died before the Lord commanded the angel to stop at the threshing floor of Ornan the Jebusite (see 1 Chron. 21:15). An angel shut the lion's mouth to save Daniel. Angels freed the apostles imprisoned for their faith (see Acts 5:19; 12:6-7). An angel told Cornelius how to find Peter in order to hear the gospel (see Acts 10:3). An angel struck judgment on wicked Herod (see Acts 12:23).

An angel encouraged Paul in a storm (see Acts 27:23). An angel ministered to Jesus in the Garden of Gethsemane.

The Nature of Angels

Angels were created by God, and yet were present with God prior to the creation of the world (see Gen. 2:1; Col. 1:16). Angels were created with free will, as evidenced by the capacity of lucifer and the angelic host of Heaven to rebel (see Isa. 14:12-15; Jude 6). Angels have supernatural discernment and wisdom (see 2 Sam. 14:17,20). They have supernatural strength (see Ps. 103:20; Matt. 28:2; 2 Pet. 2:11), the capacity to manifest themselves in physical form as God may will (see Gen. 19:1-3; Heb. 13:2), and the ability to transcend physical confinements of our material world such as time, space, and the visible elements (see Rev. 10:1-3). Angels are limited (as created beings) to what authority God gives them (see Matt. 24:36; 1 Pet. 1:12). They do not reproduce (see Matt. 22:30), and are never to be worshipped (see Col. 2:18-19; Rev. 22:8-9).

Kinds of Angels

The Bible refers to different types of angels who also appear to have differing functions. This list is not meant to be exhaustive, but let us look at some various forms of angels.

Archangels—The word archangel means to be "first in political rank or power," indicating that this is the highest rank of heavenly hosts. Scripture calls Michael an archangel (see Jude 9). He had a kind of warrior anointing about him as evidenced in his warring with the Prince of Persia (see Dan. 10:13), and contending with the devil saying *"The Lord rebuke you!"* (see Jude 9). He also has a special role coming up in the last days and seems to have a protective role over the Jewish people: *"At that time Michael shall stand up, the great prince who stands watch over the sons of your people"* (Dan. 12:1).

Scriptures does not call Gabriel an archangel, but it is assumed he is, since he is prominent in the Bible and because his name is derived from a root word meaning "strength" or "chief," which is characteristic of archangels. The poet John Milton called Gabriel an archangel in a poem, which culturally popularized the thought that he was one. Gabriel came with messages from Heaven, particularly around the time of the birth of John and Jesus.

Cherubim—The first biblical reference to the cherubim is in Genesis 3:24. They were posted at the east of the Garden of Eden (as well as a flaming sword) to guard the way to the garden and to the Tree of Life. Adam and Eve had been banished from the Garden after the fall, and these beings were to guard the entrance.

The word "cherubim" in Hebrew is *keruvim*, and they are mentioned 90 times in the Old Testament. Cherubim of gold, made by Moses, were to be placed at either end of the Ark of the Covenant. They faced one another over the mercy seat in the middle and their wings were outstretched covering the mercy seat (see Exod. 25:18-22). They were also seen by Ezekiel in their place in Heaven appearing with eyes all around, and beside them were *"wheels within wheels."* They had four faces: the face of a cherub, a man, a lion and an eagle. They also have wings (see Ezek. 10).

The cherubim are only mentioned once in the New Testament, in Hebrews 9:5, where reference is made of their previous function on the mercy seat, calling them *"cherubim of glory."* Indeed the cherubim seemed to have an Old Testament function as guardians of the glory of the Lord. They exemplified this in the Garden of Eden, on the Ark of the Covenant, and a likeness of them was sewn into the curtain that separates the Holy Place from the Most Holy Place (see 2 Chron. 3:14) and as heavenly guardians (see Ezek. 1, 10).

The role of the cherubim may have changed in the New Testament. Jesus' death caused the curtain in the Holy of Holies to be torn in two. We, the believer, are to be carriers of the glory of the Lord. The cherubim seem still linked to the Glory realm but not in the Ark, Garden of Eden, or temple.

Seraphim—The root of "seraphim" is the verb *seraph*, which means "to set on fire, to burn." The seraphim are known as burning, fiery, gliding angelic beings of a fiery color, or flame-like in appearance. In Isaiah 6 we see that Isaiah saw the seraphim above the throne of God. They had six wings: two to cover their face, two to cover their feet, and two to fly with. The seraphim cry out *"Holy, holy, holy is the Lord of hosts; the whole earth is full of His glory!"* (Isa. 6:3).

The seraphim are positioned above the throne of God. They seem to have a function of glorifying God and possibly as His "personal attendants." One of the seraphim flew to Isaiah, having a live coal from the altar in his hand. The angel touched Isaiah's mouth with the coal, saying: *"Behold, this has touched your lips; your iniquity is taken away, and your sin is purged."* Then the Lord spoke: *"Whom shall I send, and who will go for Us?"* Isaiah replied, *"Here am I! Send me."* The Lord said, *"Go, and tell this people...."* (Isa. 6:6-9).

Guardian Angels—When our daughter Gabrielle was three years old, I heard a loud crash coming from her bedroom. I ran to her assistance to find her large dresser drawer overturned on the floor. But she was perched on top of a bunk bed, completely safe. When I asked her what happened, she told me in her sweet toddler voice that she was attempting to climb the dresser when it began to topple. Suddenly, unseen hands picked her up and placed her on the top of the bunk bed safely out of harm's way. What compounded the strangeness of this story is that I heard on the local news the same week this happened, another three-year-old girl was climbing her bedroom dresser when it fell on top of her, killing her. I do not understand why that happened. I do believe an angel protected my little daughter, even as I pray for protection for her and our other children on a daily basis.

Scripture definitely alludes to the fact that all believers in Jesus have angels who help fulfill roles of protection, and yet the term "guardian angel" is never biblically used. Matthew 18:10 says, *"Take heed that you do not despise one of these little ones, for I say to you that in heaven their angels always see the face of My Father who is in heaven."* Notice the mention of *"their angels,"* indicating we have angels assigned specifically to us.

When Peter was supernaturally released from prison and stood knocking at the door, Rhoda told the disciples Peter was there. They didn't believe it at first, saying, *"It must be his angel"* (Acts 12:15). It was accepted in the early church that we each have at least one angel assigned to us.

Some more biblical references to the protective role angels play in our lives are found in Psalm 34:7, *"The angel of the Lord encamps all around those who fear Him, and delivers them."* Also, Psalm 91:11-12: *"For He shall give His angels charge over you, to keep you in all your ways. In their hands they shall bear you up, lest you dash your feet against a stone."* Lastly, Hebrews 1:14 states, *"Are they not all ministering spirits sent forth to minister for those who will inherit salvation?"*

Our son Judah was around five years old when he ran to John and my bedroom one night in great fear. He had seen in his room, with his natural eyes, a green snake. Suddenly a white light came out of Heaven, devouring the green snake. Needless to say, we didn't completely understand the meaning of this encounter, but believed the Lord was protecting our son. A week later, while visiting my husband's parents, Judah was outside playing in the snow while my father-in-law removed snow with a powerful, bladed snowblower. Unwisely, he left the snowblower going while he got something in the house, leaving Judah outside with the snowblower. The blower caught ahold of the end of Judah's scarf, wrapped around his neck, and was wrapping it around the blades, dragging Judah's face nearer the blades when at the last moment, it mysteriously stopped. Judah was completely safe. We cannot prove a connection with the strange nighttime encounter, but in our hearts, we believe an angel was sent to thwart a demonic plan to harm our son.

Canada's Highway 401 stretches for 828 kilometers. The area passing through Toronto is the busiest highway in the world and one of the widest.[42] Before I was married, I was driving in the passing (left) lane of this highway at 120 km per hour, surrounded by cars in front, behind, and to my right. Then I heard the pop of a blown right front tire and felt the jerk of the wheel pulling my car into the right lane beside me, which was full of cars similarly moving at fast speeds. I knew I was in trouble. The next moment, I was completely stopped, safely on the right shoulder of the highway. I sat trembling, wondering how I could get from the far left lane, across three lanes of busy traffic to be stopped safely on the right shoulder, completely stopped and safe. I knew it was a miracle of angelic intervention. I later learned my sister had been awakened out of a deep sleep just before I was in this predicament. She was prompted to pray for my safety.

Angels in Human Form—Hebrews 13:2 states, *"Do not forget to entertain strangers, for by so doing some have unwittingly entertained angels."*

Nancy Ravenhill, daughter-in-law of well-known evangelist and author, Leonard Ravenhill wrote in her book, *Touched by Heaven*, of a time when a couple visited her parents while she was away on her freshman year of college. They were believed to be from Bethany Bible College. The kind couple prayed for and encouraged her parents. They also left a brochure of Bethany Bible College with her parents, stating they were a part of the school and felt strongly that Nancy should be given the information. Her parents lived in California and the Bible school was in Minnesota. When Nancy obtained the brochure, she immediately knew it was the school for her. She enrolled, met her future husband there and her ministry was launched at that school. When she inquired at this school about this couple describing them from what her parents had told her, she was told no one known at the school met that description.[43]

The ministry of angels on earth and in Heaven is alive and well—whether they are unseen to us or seen in the spirit realm or in human form. There is no biblical precedence for praying to angels, telling them what to do, and certainly not worshipping them. What we can do is thank God for them, ask for the ability to see in that realm, position ourselves to see what is there, and give glory to God in it all.

SEEING IN THE HEAVENLY REALMS

We have positional access to heavenly realms. We are raised to sit together in the heavenly places in Christ Jesus (see Eph. 2:6), our citizenship is in Heaven (see Phil. 3:20), and we are to seek those things and set our mind on the things which are above, where Christ is (see Col. 3:1-2).

Notice from Ephesians 2 the plural *"places"* is referenced in terms of Heaven. In other words, there appears to be more than one place in Heaven. For example, the throne room (see Rev. 4), the New Jerusalem (see Rev. 21), the River of Life and Tree of Life (see Rev. 22), the books including the Book of Life in Heaven (see Rev. 20:12) and I believe there is a meadow or place of natural beauty in Heaven as possibly described in Psalm 23.

The Apostle Paul recounts an encounter he had within the third Heaven (see 2 Cor. 12:1-4). The third Heaven refers to the highest Heaven, where the Father dwells (see Rev. 4), and the full measure of the Presence of God (see Heb. 9:24).

The second Heaven, which has no direct reference in the Bible, is often referred to as the operating realm of satan and his demons. Ephesians 6:12 refers to this realm saying, *"For we do not wrestle against flesh and blood, but against principalities, against powers, against the rulers of the darkness of this age, against spiritual hosts of wickedness in the heavenly places."*

Finally, the first Heaven is the firmament, earth's atmosphere and where we dwell (see Gen. 1:14).

Like the Apostle Paul, as well as numerous other biblical characters including Ezekiel, Isaiah, Daniel and John, we can have encounters in the third Heaven. They would not be as common as seeing pictures or visions, but nonetheless are available for believers.

Cloud of Witnesses

One day I was spending time with the Lord, when suddenly I felt my spirit ascend while my body was still on earth. I could see into heavenly realms, noting a group of people whom I immediately knew were my ancestors who had gone on to Heaven. I saw my grandmother, whom I knew on earth. She had died some ten years before this experience. I was very overwhelmed, thinking, "I'm not dead yet, but I can see into this realm. Wow!" I do not know how communication happened exactly, but I heard my family members say to me, "You are Patricia. We are cheering you on. Our race is over on earth but you have the capacity to bring light into dark places. Tell them of this place, and tell them He is worth it all. He is worth it all. He is worth it all." I knew they spoke of Jesus. When I was back on earth, in spirit and body, I began to weep. This encounter changed my focus in many ways. I asked the Lord to help every day that I live and every breath that I breathe to be lived for His glory.

Another day, I was playing my guitar and spending time loving Jesus when suddenly, by the spirit, I was in what I think was the throne room. In the spirit (my body still on earth and still playing the guitar), I walked forward toward the Lord seated on the throne as He beckoned me forward. I sat on His lap and the throne seemed to turn into a rocking chair as my Heavenly Father held me close. He then began to sing a song over me, which on earth I began to play on my guitar and sing. It went on in perfect rhyme for about 20 minutes. It was about His Father love for me. The song was healing, and the encounter forever solidified my view of God as my Father.

One day I positioned myself to see into heavenly realms, unlike the previous encounters, which were not initiated on my part. As I sought to see in the heavenly realms, I distinctly remember feeling I was going somewhere in the spirit; I also sensed that I had the choice to go with it—or shut it off. I asked the Lord to lead me and sought to press on. I then felt in the spirit I was on streets of transparent, pure gold. I saw great light, beauty, and a gate of pearl. Yet I did not go far in or enter this celestial city. I was marveling over the fact that I was allowed to see this, when I heard what I believe to be the voice of an angel. He said, "Your name is in the Book of Life. Therefore, you are allowed to be here." That was it. No further words. Soon after, I was back in "normal mode."

Later, I reread Revelation 21:27, speaking of the New Jerusalem, *"But there shall by no means enter it anything that defiles, or causes an abomination or a lie, but only those who are written in the Lamb's Book of Life."* The fact that my name (and yours, if you are a believer and follower of Jesus) is presently written in the Lamb's Book of Life and not just in the "sweet by and by" was enlightening to me.

Chapter 11

EXPRESSIONS OF THE PROPHETIC

*T*he prophetic can be expressed in many ways, including in personal prophecy (prophesying over an individual), corporate prophetic words (giving a prophetic word in a church or meeting), prophetic painting (paintings created out of the prompting of the Lord), prophetic music (sounds inspired divinely), prophetic songs (songs sung for that moment inspired by the Lord), prophetic dance (sometimes intercessory in nature or expressions of intimacy), prophetic evangelism (combining prophecy with evangelism), prophetic intercession (praying what is on the heart of God), prophetic creativity (sculptures, designs, poems or other creative expressions), prophetic preaching, and I'm sure there are many other prophetic assertions. We will look more in-depth at some.

PERSONAL PROPHECY

Prophetic etiquette must be applied to personal prophecy to ensure the gift is used to bless and not diminish individuals.

Loving the individual is more important than giving a profound prophetic word. First Corinthians 13:2 says, *"And though I have the gift of prophecy, and understand all mysteries and all knowledge, and though I have all faith, so that I could remove mountains, but have not love, I am nothing."* If the individual does not experience the love of God in a word given, it is much better to not have given the word.

The Bible makes clear that prophecy is to edify, encourage, and comfort (see 1 Cor. 14:3,4,12,26), and thus words are to reflect the life-giving nature of God. Even in conviction or correction from the Lord, one is edified to reach higher in the hope for positive change. If a prophetic person is seeing a negative pattern or sin in a person's life, it is not for them to call out that sin. However, with the right wording, the negative prophetically seen can be "flipped to the positive." For example, if you see a spirit of anger on someone, it could be declared, "The Lord is giving you patience, temperance, and more of the fruit of the spirit."

Dear friends of ours, Chester and Betsy Kylstra, told us a story of receiving a long prophetic word from an internationally known prophet that left them feeling very encouraged. When they played the recording later, they realized the prophet had brought much correction to them. He had just worded it in such a way and operated in an anointing of love, grace, and encouragement. They were left with knowing God wanted some change in their lives, but that it was out of His overwhelming love for them.

It has been said; do not prophesy dates, mates, and babies. There is particular truth to that for those operating in a gift of prophecy and for those starting out in learning how to prophesy, as opposed to an office of a prophet. In other words, do not prophesy that such and such an event will happen by a certain date, and you will get married to so and so, and one will give birth to a baby. These kinds of words, if they don't come to pass, can be very discouraging. However, I have seen these kinds of words be given by gifted prophets with accuracy and anointing, and the words have come to pass—so we cannot apply this rule to all. Such words were also given in the Bible.

It is helpful to start with a scripture and launch from that place with revelation from the Word in giving personal prophecy. I know of ministries that require their prophetic people to prophesy first out of scripture. Either way, starting with a scripture or not, it is important that the word aligns with the Word of God.

We do not need to raise the volume of our voice or manifest wildly to give some sort of credence to the word. It is also not necessary to use King James language to sound more "official." Additionally, I would add, we don't need to say, "Thus says the Lord." That phrase seems to say that the word does not need to be subject to any judgment because, "God said it." I find it more helpful to say something like, "I sense…" or, "I believe the Lord is saying…." Just be "naturally supernatural" in your delivery of a prophetic word. There is no need to be weird.

Some giving words prefer to close their eyes while prophesying so as to stay focused on the Lord and the flow of His words. Others prefer to prophesy with eyes open. That is a personal preference, and I see no hard and fast rule on that.

Prophetic Protocol

Prophetic words given to individuals should be given in proper protocol. For example, approaching someone in the parking lot of the church to give a word if one is not given permission to prophesy in the church is not honoring the leadership of that church. We want to remain in submission to authority as prophetic people. If we do have a word for someone, do ask the person if it is okay for you to share that word. The only time I do not adhere to this rule is in prophetic evangelism, where I often will launch into a word I'm getting for a person, as they often do not know what prophesy is in the first place.

Direction words should not be given if one is learning prophetic ministry. And when given, they should be given with humility and be subject to judgment and not given with a spirit of control. One could say, "I'm sensing there will be a connection for you with the country of Israel. Does that make any sense to you?" Or, "I see a picture of you teaching children the ways of God." That is better than, "You will be teaching children." Similarly, "I sense the Lord has given you creative gifts, and I believe you will walk in anointing in the creative arts." That is more acceptable than, "You are supposed to paint."

If it is later proven you are incorrect in a prophetic word given, it is important to take ownership for the word, repent where necessary and ask for forgiveness. If someone comes to you later to ask for more explanation or clarity of the word, time should be taken to do so.

It is best for words to be recorded, thus enabling those who receive the word to be able to listen to it later, subject it to their leaders for judgment, and also as a safeguard for the person giving the word to know the word they gave cannot be misinterpreted if it is recorded for review at a later time. I know of some who will not give a word unless it is recorded.

Delivered in Love

Delivering personal prophetic words in an attitude of love, humility, and teachability is most welcome and can be used of the Lord to bless many. If you practice prophesying over people, you will grow in it. One guy I know wanted to grow in personal prophesy, so he emailed many on his email database and asked them to email him back if they wanted to receive a prophetic word from him. He wanted to practice his prophetic gift and thought this may be a clever way to do so. Each day, he would email out prophetic words to those who responded to the affirmative, and he grew tremendously in the prophetic gift.

Practicing the Prophetic

We can all prophesy, according to First Corinthians 14. Remember, prophecy is about tapping into God's thoughts (see Ps. 139:17-18; Ps. 40:5), which are very numerous.

Below are some exercises that can be used to get started in "priming the pump" of prophetic revelation for an individual:

- Ask the Lord for a scripture that may be relevant for the person at this time.
- Ask the Lord for a picture for this person and the interpretation for the picture.
- What character from the Bible is the Lord highlighting for this person, and why?
- What is the Lord saying about their destiny or future?
- In what area is the Lord giving this person victory in right now?

- What is the Lord showing you about them (word of knowledge) that you would not know by any natural means?

- What is the Lord saying to them regarding relationships (family, friends, leaders, co-workers)?

- What is the Lord highlighting to you about this person's gifting or spiritual gift?

PROPHETIC PREACHING

Paul said in First Corinthians 2:4-5, *"And my speech and my preaching were not with persuasive words of human wisdom, but in demonstration of the Spirit and of power, that your faith should not be in the wisdom of men but in the power of God."* Paul spoke with apostolic authority, prophetic wisdom, and in the demonstration of the Spirit's backing.

Have you listened to a sermon or preaching that lacks the element of the Spirit? By contrast, if you have listened to a sermon or preaching where there is a connection of the Spirit, you are stirred; you know this is not just touching your brain but something of the anointing, the "umph" of the Spirit is accompanying the words.

Go With the Flow

The definition of prophetic preaching would be something like this: biblically based preaching that utilizes the prophetic gift to speak a "now" word from the Lord. The message usually is initiated by revelation from the Lord. It is authoritative in nature, often contains a call to action, often results in breakthrough, and empowers the church.

Prophetic preachers will often go with a flow of the Spirit while speaking. That is not to say they do not use notes or have structure. It is more that they will go with the spontaneous, Holy

Spirit-initiated thoughts that come while speaking, trusting the leadership of the Lord. The apostles speak in Acts 4:20 saying, *"We cannot but speak the things which we have seen and heard."*

It is not to say prophetic preaching is superior to other forms of preaching. It may just be different, and is perhaps more welcomed in churches that have a culture of honor for the prophetic.

Foundation in the Word

Prophetic preachers must ensure they have a rich foundation in the Word of God and continue to study and grow in the knowledge of the Word. It is not "either/or" for Spirit or Word; it is "both/and." The ideas on what to preach on may come from what the Lord is teaching the preacher at that point in time, from a dream, vision or other form of revelatory realm; but it must be solidly founded and backed by the Word of God. As my husband has said in regards to the Word of God, "If it is not in you, it won't come out of you." Let us get the Word of God into us.

Prophetic preachers often do not like to start speaking straight out of an announcement time. They would prefer to pray, to come out of a worship song, start with giving prophetic words, minister corporate healing or have a time of singing or praying in tongues. Heidi Baker, American missionary to Africa, often will sing before she speaks. You can tell she is trying to get in a flow with the Holy Spirit in her speaking.

Jesus seasoned His preaching with stories, analogies, and colorful images. Prophetic preaching will similarly utilize creativity in stories.

Calls for a Response

Prophetic preaching tends to end with an opportunity for response on behalf of the people. Hearts can be stirred, and an opportunity to receive prayer into what the message stirs in the person is important. It enables the receiver to take ownership for the message. They may come forward in response to a call, to receive prayer, or simply to stand before the Lord in obedience. Similarly, they may choose to respond to the Lord in their hearts, right there in their seats. Regardless, giving an opportunity to respond to the message helps lead to lasting heart change.

Growing as a Prophetic Preacher

I have listened to many sermons given by John Arnott. Years ago I asked him how he could speak with such anointing, authority, and skill. His response was, "Well, you do it, then you do it again, and then you do it again and again." Truly the exercising of the ability to speak is an important part of growth. Seasoned preachers should give opportunities for those growing in the gift. Often speaking in smaller group settings, on weekend retreats, or speaking in the youth and kids' ministries are good opportunities to grow in the gift.

When I was in grade seven, I was asked by my teacher in the new Christian school I started to attend, to read a passage of scripture to the class. I stood up to speak and my insecurities surfaced; my mouth went dry and I could not get a word out of my mouth. I sat down, red-faced and embarrassed. The enemy used that incident for years to convince me I could not speak in public. When times came for me to speak publically, I somehow got out of it. That was until I repented before the Lord for believing that lie, broke my agreement with it, and forgave myself for the embarrassing grade-seven incident. Now I speak often without fear and know God will lead and back me.

Biblical Prophetic Preaching

An example of biblical prophetic preaching would be when the Holy Spirit was poured out at Pentecost in Acts 2. The people were amazed, perplexed, and some were mocking when the Holy Spirit came as a wind and as tongues of fire, causing a spiritual drunkenness in the people. Peter got up and preached a powerful prophetic message. It was the "this is that" message, referring to the prophecy of Joel 2. He also quoted David from Psalm 16 and 68. His depth of the Word comes through as he receives revelation that this is what Joel, Jesus, and David had all prophesied. Peter delivered his message with boldness, giving stories of Jesus' miracle-working power, and confronting the people on their blindness regarding Jesus. What was the response? Acts 2:37 says, *"When they heard this, they were cut to the heart."* Peter then gave them an opportunity to respond by saying: *"Repent, and let every one of you be baptized In the name of Jesus Christ"* (Acts 2:38).. Those who gladly received his word were baptized, and that day about 3,000 souls were added to them.

Another example is recorded in Acts 4. Peter and John had been arrested, and they gave an address to the Sanhedrin and religious leaders. Acts 4:8 records, *"Then Peter, filled with the Holy Spirit said to them...."* Preaching prophetically is greatly enhanced by preaching full—full of the Holy Spirit. It is the Holy Spirit who speaks to us and preaching prophetically is His speaking through us.

Stephen's address in Acts 7 is also a great example of prophetic preaching. He gets revelation from the Lord, using scriptures, stories and explanations as he speaks. He even sees into the heavens as he is preaching. What was the response? Interestingly, it is the same phrase used for Peter's sermon: *"They were cut to the heart"* (Acts 7:54). This passage however records a different kind of "cut to the heart," as they gnashed at him with their teeth—and then they stoned Stephen to death. Angels are released in prophetic preaching to do the bidding of the Lord. Demons are stirred or evicted as well.

Jesus' Sermon on the Mount recorded in Matthew 5-7 was also prophetic preaching at it's best. He simply opened His mouth and all that wisdom came out. He used scriptures saying He did not come to destroy the law or the prophets but to fulfill them. He uses analogies such as God caring for the birds and the lilies to show that worry will not help but God will care for all of us. The response was the people were astonished. What an example of a connection with the Spirit and going with a flow!

Chapter 12

WALKING IN FULFILLED PROPHECY

*P*ersonal prophecy is conditional upon our response. Similarly, prophesy over a church, city, or nation is conditional upon the collective response of the people therein. We can say yes or we can say no to invitations from God.

In the context of the parables of the workers in the vineyard and the wedding feast in Matthew 20 and 22 respectively, Jesus ends with this remark, *"For many are called, but few are chosen"* (Matt. 22:14). In other words, the call or invitation to come into salvation and into fullness of Heaven's destiny is wide. However, few choose to pay the price, walk the walk, and fulfill their divine calling.

There are prophecies that are unconditional and will be fulfilled as the Lord has ordained. For example, there are 300 Old Testament references to the Messiah's first coming. Jesus fulfilled every one of them, even very specific words such as He would be from the tribe of Judah (prophesied in Genesis 49:10; fulfilled Luke 3:33); He was heir to the throne of David (prophesied Isaiah 9:7; fulfilled Luke 1:32-33); His birthplace in Bethlehem (prophesied Micah 5:2; fulfilled Luke 2:4-5,7); born of a virgin (prophesied Isaiah 7:14; fulfilled Luke 1:26-27, 30-31). There are 2400 different references in the Bible to the end times and Jesus' Second Coming. All of those will come to pass.

Yet, the prophesies over your life and mine are conditional on us—our agreement, our walk with God, our obedience. We can see stories of both fulfilled and unfulfilled destines in the lives of biblical characters.

Solomon

Solomon would be an example of someone who walked initially in fulfillment of the call of God on his life but he did not finish well.

The Lord actually appeared to Solomon twice. The first time he appeared to him in a dream and asked Solomon what he wanted (see 1 Kings 3:5). Solomon had replied he wanted an understanding (the word literally means "hearing") heart to judge or lead the people. The Lord was pleased with such a request and gave Solomon not only that great wisdom, but also riches and honor. The second appearance is recorded in 1 Kings 9 after the temple is completed and Solomon dedicates it to the Lord. Here the Lord spells out the necessary price of obedience.

> *Now if you walk before Me as your father David walked, in integrity of heart and in uprightness, to do according to all that I have commanded you, and if you keep My statutes and My judgments, then I will establish the throne of your kingdom over Israel forever, as I promised David your father, saying, "You shall not fail to have a*

man on the throne of Israel." But if you or your sons at all turn from following Me, and do not keep My commandments and My statutes which I have set before you, but go and serve other gods and worship them, then I will cut off Israel from the land which I have given them; and this house which I have consecrated for My name I will cast out of My sight (1 Kings 9:4-7).

Sadly, even though the Lord appeared twice to Solomon, gave him wisdom, blessings, and honor, Solomon's heart turned away from the Lord. He had 700 wives and 300 concubines, which he *"clung to these in love"* (1 Kings 11:2-3). These women, many of whom worshipped false gods, turned away his heart from the Lord; he went after other gods and *"his heart was not loyal to the Lord his God, as was the heart of his father David"* (1 Kings 11:4).

The Lord became angry with Solomon and this was the downfall of the Davidic dynasty. Ahijah prophesies over Jeroboam, Solomon's servant, that he will be given ten of the twelve tribes of Israel, as the kingdom will be torn away from Solomon's son. When Solomon's son Rehoboam comes to power, indeed he is wicked, the people revolt and ten of the tribes of Israel go under the leadership of Jeroboam. The other two (Judah and Benjamin) remain under Solomon's lineage until all were taken away to Babylon.

It has been said that the three most common traps that derail men in ministry are, "the girls, the gold, and the glory." This highlights the critical importance of our hearts being first and completely devoted to the Lord.

FULFILLED PROPHECIES

Let's look at some stories of fulfilled prophecies.

Randy Clark

Randy Clark was the man used of God to help spark revival in Toronto on January 20, 1994. Previous to this, Randy had had many failures in his life. These included his first marriage, a pastorate he was dismissed from, and people he prayed for who did not get healed. However, he did have some powerful prophetic words over his life including one from John Wimber, former leader of the Vineyard Movement. When John first met Randy, the Lord showed John that Randy was going to be powerfully used of God to travel the world and rise up as an apostolic leader. Randy was barely surviving financially and was not at all living this word.

Later he joined the Vineyard movement and started a church in St. Louis. Randy traveled to Tulsa and then also Lakeland to Rodney Howard-Browne meetings where he received prayer numerous times. Upon his return, he was at a regional Vineyard meeting and the Holy Spirit used him to impact many of the leaders. John Arnott heard about this and invited Randy to come to Toronto.

Before traveling to Toronto, Randy admits he was scared. He didn't know if the Holy Spirit was going to show up and he felt afraid of going there only to disappoint John and the Toronto church. His fear continued right until the night before he left. That's when a prophetic friend called him (who didn't know Randy was going to Toronto) and said, "The Lord says, 'Test me, test me, test me for I will surely back you.'" At that moment, all the fear left. Randy just knew God was going to come through and do something in Toronto. He didn't realize the magnitude of it: those four day of meetings turned into 12 years of nightly meetings. Randy was there for 42 days instead of four as the Holy Spirit came in such power night after night. That move of the Spirit, of which my husband and I are a part, is still going on to this day. Randy Clark lived and is living the prophetic words over his life even as he travels the world as a healing evangelist.[44]

Heidi Baker

Heidi Baker gives the example in her life of a prophecy she received through Randy Clark while she was in Toronto. It was such a powerful experience; she was knocked to the floor under the power of the Spirit and actually remained incapacitated by the Spirit for days. I remember Heidi being carried in and out of meetings and even to the bathroom via a wheelchair. The Lord prophesied to her that He was giving her the nation of Mozambique and then would give her other nations (as in multitudes would be saved, healed, and delivered by the Holy Spirit's power through her). At that time they had 300 orphans, three churches, and a few buildings in Maputo. Heidi and Rolland Baker were basically burned out missionaries and Heidi jokes that she was contemplating getting a job at Kmart.

You would think after such a powerful prophetic word and with amazing signs following, they would see the Heavens open upon their return to Mozambique.

Actually, all hell broke loose. An opposing group took their buildings from them, the large U.S. church that was poised to give them 1 million dollars in a donation withdrew it because they found out they had been to that "Toronto church." On top of that a mysterious illness affected Heidi and devastating floods hit Mozambique.

But Rolland and Heidi didn't give up; instead they pressed into believing that prophetic word. After the floods, revival broke out and thousands of people wanted a Bible and to hear the gospel. Churches sprang up to the tune of now over 11,000 churches have started under their ministry. They are feeding and educating 7,000 orphans and have centers in many other nations such as Malawi,

South Africa, Sudan, and India. The word came to pass although it was tested.[45]

My Prophetic Journey

I had many prophetic words about missions, traveling the nations, and leading many to Jesus since I was a child. Since I did not know any women in ministry when I grew up, I thought I would become a doctor to help fulfill the prophecies. I was a straight A student in high school and started university as a pre-medical student, overloading my schedule with Physics, Calculus, Biology, Organic Chemistry, and Psychology. I'll never forget that first semester. I failed my first test ever, a Calculus test. I was devastated. All those unhealed hurts and insecurities came to the surface in me. I finished the year, transferred to the college nursing program, later received a Bachelor of Science in Nursing, and worked in that field. John and I married and I gave up nursing when I had our first child, our son Judah. I died to the dream of missions and ministry. I was a stay-at-home Mom with a husband who was a bank manager.

John had also received many prophetic words of ministry and serving the Lord full time, and he had a strong calling as a pastor. He had been through Bible school and was pastoring many of his banking customers. The district manager would question John as to why there were customers crying in his office when it was supposed to be about mortgages, Registered Retirement Savings Accounts, and trust accounts.

I implored the Lord how we could turn prophecy into fulfillment. I actually didn't need more prophetic words at that point; I needed to know how to walk in fulfillment. The Lord taught me some lessons in walking in fulfilled prophecy. God resurrected the dreams in His way, in His time. Even now, I am walking in prophecies given to me when I was eight years old.

KEYS TO WALKING IN FULFILLED PROPHECY

Let us look at some of the important aspects to walking in destiny.

Believe—Luke 1:45 says, *"Blessed is she who believed, for there will be a fulfillment of those things which were told her from the Lord."* Once you judge the prophetic words you have received and feel a confirmation that they are indeed from the Lord, you need to believe and walk in faith. Faith is the currency of Heaven. Reread the "hall of faith" in Hebrews 11, as those heroes of the faith walked in their destiny through faith.

Decree—Proverbs 18:21 says, *"Death and life are in the power of the tongue."* Job 22:28 says, *"You will also declare a thing, and it will be established for you; so light will shine on your ways."* The agreement of our mind and mouth with the Word of the Lord is powerful in walking in fulfilled destiny. (See "Prophetic Decrees" in the section on prayer.)

Obey and Act—James 1:22 says, *"But be doers of the word, and not hearers only, deceiving yourselves."* John 15:10 says, *"If you keep my commandments, you will abide in My love."* What the Lord tells you to do, do it. Take action steps, take faith steps when there is a confirmed word of the Lord. You can't do God's part, but He won't do your part.

Our daughter Aquila was five years old when she had a nudging from the Holy Spirit to pursue learning the French language. I bought the language program Rosetta Stone in French for levels 1, 2, and 3. Aquila devoured them and also sought out French tutors through the years. Aquila married a Swiss national whose first language is French, and she teaches English at a French Christian School in Geneva, Switzerland. Indeed, Aquila acted on prophetic revelation and is reaping the benefits of that obedience.

STEWARD THE WORD

Stewardship is about being faithful with what one is given. In that place of trustworthiness, more will be entrusted. Luke 16:10-12 states, *"He who is faithful in what is least is faithful also in much; and he who is unjust in what is least is unjust also in much. Therefore if you have not been faithful in the unrighteous mammon, who will commit to your trust the true riches? And if you have not been faithful in what is another man's, who will give you what is your own?"* I have seen those who want their own company or their own ministry—and are not willing to serve time apprenticing under someone else who is functioning in the role they desire. Be willing to take the low position, serve, volunteer, be an "Elisha to Elijah," and see the Lord open future doors and pour out a double portion upon you.

Before time began, God called us and gave us a purpose as Second Timothy 1:9 states: *"[God] has saved us and called us with a holy calling, not according to our works, but according to His own purpose and grace which was given to us in Christ Jesus before time began."* As we see from this passage, grace is given to us to walk into His purpose for us.

Five Signs to Know Your Calling

Recently I heard a speaker by the name of Robert Henderson share five signs in knowing specifics of your calling:

You will enjoy what you do. If you don't initially like what God has called you to do, if it is of Him, He will change your heart to enjoy it.

You will be gifted at what you are called to do. Grace is given to us for what we are called to do, and gifts are attached to that grace.

You will have success doing what God calls you to do. In other words, you will be fruitful in it; and as you are faithful with little, more will be given.

You will be able to make money doing what you are gifted to do. God wants you to make a living doing what you are passionate about. This may not happen right way and volunteering is important at times but eventually, you will be able to be financially supported in your God-given calling.

The right people will bear witness to what you are called to do. In other words, you will receive confirmation from those God has placed in your life to speak into your life.

WHEN YOU STRUGGLE

Some may assert that they have not received a clear word from the Lord and don't know what to do.

We all have the written Word of God, which is full of revelation for us. Continuing to dig into the Word of God is crucial, as we will see in the next section. Additionally, what are desires inside of you? What do you like to do? I'm convinced God never ordained anyone to hate their jobs. No matter one's occupation, may it be done unto the Lord and with joy in one's heart. First Corinthians 10:31 says, *"Therefore…whatever you do, do all to the glory of God."* Nehemiah 8:10 says, *"…for the joy of the Lord is your strength."*

Additionally, trying some different endeavors can be helpful. Joyce Meyer says that before she became a speaker, she tried to serve God by working in the children's ministry at her church. She was not particularly given grace for such ministry and was actually dismissed from that role. Perhaps it was a sign from God for her! She realized she did like to talk though, and had a way with words.

She began to lead a small Bible study in her home. From that place, her Bible teaching ministry was launched.

Chapter 13

PROPHETIC EVANGELISM

here are two clear directives the Lord has given all of us as believers in Jesus. One is the Great Commandment—to love Him with all our hearts and all that we are; and on the heels of that, to love ourselves and love others (see Matt. 22:37-40). The second is the Great Commission, recorded in each of the gospels. In Matthew 28:18-20 Jesus said, *"All authority has been given to Me in Heaven and on earth. Go therefore and make disciples of all the nations, baptizing them in the name of the Father and of the Son and of the Holy Spirit, teaching them to observe all things that I have commanded you; and lo, I am with you always, even to the end of the age."*

Mark records it this way:

> *Go into all the world and preach the gospel to every creature. He who believes and is baptized will be saved; but he who does not believe will be condemned. And these*

145

*signs will follow those who believe: In My name they will
cast out demons; they will speak with new tongues; they
will take up serpents; and if they drink anything deadly,
it will by no means hurt them; they will lay hands on the
sick, and they will recover* (Mark 16:15-18).

No matter your personality type, your gifts mix, or your job, if
you are a believer in Jesus, this is your commission. You are drafted
as a worker in the harvest.

How I Became an Evangelist

I used to believe a lie that my function in the body of Christ
was to be a prophetic person and a pastor alongside my husband.
I figured I'd leave the job of evangelism up to the evangelists. The
Lord shattered that lie.

Many years ago, I was speaking at a prophetic conference in
Ottawa. I was on my way to speak at one of the sessions when
we passed a group of young people sitting out on the street. They
looked "interesting," with spiked hair, tattoos, and piercings in
unusual places. They seemed to be just passing the time, smoking, chatting, and doing nothing. I had an overwhelming urge to
go and speak to those young people. I did not want to go into this
church to talk to these Christian people about prophecy anymore.
I wanted to stay out on the streets prophesying over these young
people. However, I was just on time for my meeting and stopping to
talk to them would mean I would be late. I walked on by that group
of young people and went to the church to speak at the meeting,
feeling a pain in my heart. Something was deposited in me that
day. I knew I had to take the prophetic gift outside the walls of
the church.

I received a challenging prophetic word in the fall of 1995. A
very prophetic gal from Indonesia was brought in to prophesy to a

group of prophetic people. This girl didn't seem to know our rules for prophecy. She had unusual manifestations and as she flopped about on the floor, she said to me something I will never forget: "Do you love souls or do you just love yourself and your ministry?" Ouch! The word may not have fit the "edify, encourage, and comfort" portfolio, but I knew it was an accurate word for me. I loved myself, and my ministry; but a great love for souls I did not carry at that time. If our ministry, our anointing, and our reputation consume us, the Lord has a way of lovingly pushing us to grow up and get past ourselves. It's about Him, it's about a Kingdom, and it's about a promise the Father made to the Son that He would have a Bride. We get to be a part of this wonderful culmination of events but it takes love.

The final push from the Lord came during meetings at Canadian Prophetic Counsel meetings in Kelowna, British Columbia where Patricia King was speaking. I actually arrived late to that session and can't tell you anything about what she said. However, after the session she did a general prayer, releasing a heart for the harvest to be unleashed. All I remember is I was suddenly overtaken by uncontrollable weeping for the souls of men to turn to the Lord. I wept for hours, leaning on some kind lady next to me who kept handing me tissues until we had to leave the building as it was closing. This was the first of four such encounters of travail for souls. After each of them, I saw a marked difference in my heart and an anointing for evangelism.

When I got home from B.C. after the Patricia King meeting, I gathered two others who were keen prophetic types and we went to the local mall. The Lord directed us to speak to two ladies with red hair. We approached them, told them God sent us to tell them He loved them, gave them some prophetic words—and they both gave their lives to Jesus. They joined our church and later, their children also gave their lives to the Lord. It was as though the Lord wanted us to have an early success to show us this really does work. Since that time we have seen so many saved, we have lost count. It has been a wonderful adventure of which I am thrilled to be a part.

By definition, prophetic evangelism is when a born-again believer receives a prophecy (prophetic word or word of knowledge) from the Holy Spirit for an unbeliever, and they seize the opportunity to win that person to Jesus. A powerful mix happens when we combine the prophetic anointing with evangelism.

Moved with Compassion

Jesus is moved with compassion for lost souls. It is love that sets the stage. It is love that opens the door. It is love that moves us to action when it comes to the harvest. If you have no love for souls, you won't make much of a harvester. Matthew 9:35-38 says:

> *"Then Jesus went about all the cities and villages, teaching in their synagogues, preaching the gospel of the kingdom, and healing every sickness and every disease among the people. But when He saw the multitudes, He was moved with compassion for them, because they were weary and scattered, like sheep having no shepherd. Then He said to His disciples, 'The harvest truly is plentiful, but the laborers are few. Therefore pray the Lord of the harvest to send out laborers into His harvest.'"*

Notice what Jesus does next, *"And when He had called His twelve disciples to Him, He gave them power over unclean spirits, to cast them out, and to heal all kinds of sickness and all kinds of disease"* (Matt. 10:1). Compassion set the stage for Him to send them out with power!

PRACTICAL TIPS ON PROPHETIC EVANGELISM

Make yourself available to the Lord to be used in prophetic evangelism. It can happen as we go about our daily business or when we purpose to go and win souls. The Lord will challenge us to go beyond our comfort zones.

Be led by the Spirit. Prior to going out on prophetic evangelism we will pray and ask the Lord for words ahead of time. He may show us where He wants us to go, a park, the mall, or downtown. We will ask also for specific words about people such as what they look like, what they are wearing, what they need for physical healing, or whatever the Lord wants to show us.

Called "Treasure Hunting" by some, being led by the Spirit both in words ahead of time and while on the streets, looking for the ones God is highlighting for us to speak to, often yields greater fruitfulness.

Smith Wigglesworth had such a great passion for souls that he would go looking for the lost in the markets when he wasn't ministering in conferences and revivals. He would wait in the market, even all morning and into the afternoon, until he saw the person that the Lord intended him to reach with the gospel. He knew the Lord would bring him to the one that was ripe and ready for the gospel. His evangelistic fervor was Spirit-led![46]

Stir up the gift within you through speaking in tongues. I have experienced times where I feel as though I'm not flowing in the Spirit while on the streets. If I will take the time to pray in tongues, I will get reoriented in the anointing of the Lord.

Consider an "ice-breaker"; sometimes getting started can be the biggest challenge. Often we will say something like, "Hi, I believe God speaks today, and I believe He gave me a word for you. Here it is…." Or, it may be helpful to explain you are practicing hearing

God's voice for others, or that you are part of a school or are from a church, and then launch into what the Lord has shown you.

Push past initial negative reactions. We have had some of the greatest breakthroughs in evangelism after pushing past some initial negative reactions from those we want to minister to. Be secure in who you are. Keep going. Don't give up!

Love, Love, Love

Most of all, we want to give away the love of God to people. God is love and when He speaks, it is loving. The world will know us by our love.

In downtown Glasgow, Scotland, we approached a group of young girls and began to speak to them. The Lord showed me this one girl in particular had a terrible relationship with her mother and had never been affirmed by a mother's love. She had lots of makeup on and actually wore a cap that had a picture of a cracked heart on it. It was definitely a prophetic sign to me of her cracked heart. As I began to speak to her, you could see tears well up in her eyes. I then sensed the Lord asking me to hug her and affirm her, as a mother would do. I asked her permission to hug her and as I did, she began to tremble uncontrollably under the power of the Holy Spirit. She was like a jackhammer vibrating, right out there in downtown Glasgow. She was being overwhelmed by the love of God. I could feel it going in to her. It was so easy to lead her to salvation as God's love had already touched her. All but one of her friends also came to know Jesus that day.

Speak to their heart. Words of knowledge about the person will help to open up their hearts. When they realize you have information about them that no one would know by natural means, it helps to pique their curiosity, open their hearts, and make way for the message of the gospel. However, we do not want to stay on words of knowledge. We need to shift into the heart.

Go for the message of the Gospel, which is a message of love. If at all possible, go for the salvation message. You may be the only Jesus they meet. You can ask them if you can lead them in a salvation prayer.

Go for the power. Pray for healing if they need healing. You can ask them to repeat this simple prayer to have them align themselves with God's will. It is not a formula, but an open door for God to come and heal. "This healing belongs to me because of what Jesus has done. I receive my healing now in Jesus' name."

Don't get into debate. It is simply a dead-end most times. Go for the Spirit, signs and wonders, and prayer. You may be asked, "If there is a God, why is there so much suffering in the world?" We can admit we don't have all the answers, but we do know the One who does have the answers.

Two by Two

Go out two by two as Jesus did went He sent out the disciples. Prophetic evangelism is not as effective if you are on your own.

If you can have intercessors praying as you are out evangelizing, even ones right with you on the streets, that is a great asset.

Follow Through

Most of all, encourage new believers to fall in love with Jesus. Tell them to talk to Him in prayer, just like they are talking to us and that He is with them wherever they go. We like to encourage them to attend a life-giving church if possible. If you can give information on a church, either your own or one close by, that is good. We like to give them a Bible, if they don't have one, and tell them to start reading in the book of John. If you can, try to connect them with someone with a heart to disciple people.

Proverbs 11:30 says, *"He who wins souls is wise."* Let us use power tools such as prophecy, healing, miracles, and most of all love to win souls for Jesus. The rewards are eternal.

Chapter 14

HEAVEN-SENT ATTIRE

When you get a job, a good boss will also give you the tools, the equipment, the information, and the training to get the job done, to help you succeed. Do you know that we have been given some job attire from our Heavenly Father to do the work He has called us to? Do you know that sometimes there is opposition to the building that the Lord is doing? Nehemiah led the people to rebuild the walls of Jerusalem with a building tool in one hand and a weapon in the other.

So what is the attire our Heavenly Boss gives us for this great commission? He knows we will encounter some opposition from demonic principalities and powers as we seek to win and mature disciples.

The blueprint for everything we need is found in Ephesians 6. First, He says to put on the belt of truth. Know what real truth is, not what our culture and world around us says. Truths such as,

A LIFESTYLE OF DIVINE ENCOUNTERS

"you are loved by your Father God" and not lies, like "you are a success only if you are attractive, brilliant, have a good job, and lots of money."

Next, put on the breastplate of righteousness. Walk away from the entanglements of this world: lusts of the flesh, greed, drunkenness, and acts of darkness. Put on obedience to God's commands. You will be well protected with a breastplate like that.

Wear on your feet the preparation of the gospel of peace. As far as it depends on you, walk in peace in your life. And know what you're talking about in this whole message of the "gospel of peace." You will be called on to share it.

Take up the shield of faith. Believe; walk not by what you see in the natural, but walk by what you see and hear in the spiritual. You've got to believe in a miracle-working, nothing-is-impossible, all-powerful God. If you do, you can extinguish all the offensive, fiery darts that come your way. Darts like the "D's" of discouragement, depression, despairing thoughts, the dangers of the devil. We overcome by faith.

Wear the hard hat of salvation. Know Him personally in your heart.

Finally, wield the sword of the Spirit. The Word of God is powerful! What does God say about that? The Word of God says that I am an overcomer in Christ Jesus. The Lord has said to go forward in His plans.

A sword left in the sheath doesn't accomplish anything. Take out that sword. Use the word of God—*logos* and *rhema*—to accomplish that which it is supposed to accomplish.

Wear your heavenly attire. It is good for both defense and offense.

Right before all of this heavenly warrior clothing in Ephesians 6, Ephesians 5 speaks of how to walk in success. It speaks of walking in love, walking in the light, and walking in wisdom—all equipment for success in our heavenly mission.

POWER TOOLS

Jesus gives this momentous job in the Great Commission, but He also gives us the tools for the job. *"But you shall receive power when the Holy Spirit has come upon you; and you shall be witnesses to Me..."* (Acts 1:8). Use the power tools you have been given. The Holy Spirit living in us is our Guide, our Friend, our Comforter, the One who speaks to us. He is our Power Source, giving us power through the Holy Spirit living in us.

When we lived in another city, a new home was built for our family. Workers used power saws and not the old back-and-forth saws. I noticed they used power nail guns and not a hammer. They didn't sit and screw a screw in the wall by hand, but they used a power drill. They didn't take a bag of cement and mix it with water by hand, but they brought in the cement truck. Power tools accomplish a lot more with less effort on our part.

There are stories of missionaries who have been on the mission field for 20 years and haven't seen one convert. Now I don't want to make light of that, because it may be that they are plowing soil that is very hard and dry. Yet when you hear stories of Heidi Baker asking for all the deaf and sick to come forward, seeing them all get healed, and then the whole village is converted in one hour, it does make you think mission work is best done with some power tools.

The Lord would like us to exert less of our own, fleshly effort, and use His power tools that were designed to get the job done. Prophetic Evangelism is an example of using a power tool to build the Kingdom of God and get on with the job of the Great Commission. We have at our disposal the power of the Holy Spirit, anointing willing vessels to prophesy and see hearts open up as a result.

First Corinthians 14:24-25 says, *"But if all prophesy, and an unbeliever or an uninformed person comes in, he is convinced by all, he is convicted by all. And thus the secrets of his heart are revealed; and so, falling down on his face, he will worship God and report that God is truly among you."* We can use the gift of prophecy to help convince the person there is a God in Heaven that loves them and knows everything about them. Then we want to bring the message of the gospel, the message of life.

John 4 records when Jesus met the Samaritan woman at the well. Jesus asks her for water, and then begins a discussion about living water. Jesus says this to her, *"You have well said, 'I have no husband,' for you have had five husbands, and the one whom you now have is not your husband; in that you spoke truly."* Immediately she says, *"Sir, I perceive that you are a prophet."* In short, due to this encounter, the woman not only believes Jesus is the Messiah but an entire town enters into a revival because of this prophetic evangelistic encounter.

In meeting Nathaniel, Jesus said to him, *"Before Philip called you, when you were under the fig tree, I saw you."* Nathaniel answered and said, *"Rabbi, You are the Son of God! You are the King of Israel!"* Nathaniel is undone by the revelation Jesus walked in. Jesus assures him, he hasn't seen anything yet. *"You shall see Heaven open, and the angels of God ascending and descending upon the Son of Man"* (John 1:43-51).

Taking It to the Streets

In Song of Solomon 3:1-5, the bride could not find her beloved until she went out into the streets to look for him. There is something about love and passion for Jesus that helps ignite the search for Him on the streets where the lost are. We find Him there.

Outside the walls of the church, we have seen the Lord's love for His people. One girl our team spoke to had cut marks all over her body. She looked emaciated and I later found out she was anorexic.

We spoke some things to her about her that only God would know. She would periodically look at her friend with big eyes like, "How do they know that?" The friend said to us, "How do you know this stuff?" We explained that it was God speaking, as He created her and knew everything about her. The girl gave her life to Jesus, took a Bible to read we gave her, and later came out to youth group.

One young man said to us as we were doing street evangelism, "I just want you to know I'm an atheist." I felt this boldness come upon me as I said, "You won't be an atheist by the time we are finished." Sure enough, the Lord gave detailed words about this man and He very happily gave his life to Jesus.

Years ago, a town nearby decided to have a party to mark the release of a new Harry Potter book. They renamed their town New Hogsmeade, a name from the book. Harry Potter paraphernalia was everywhere, and people came out dressed as witches and wizards. We obtained permission from town authorities to set up a "Spiritual Readings" booth. It was a phenomenal time as around 20 people gave their lives to Jesus. We had a line up for our booth and some of our team members were also on the streets prophesying over individuals. They particularly saw young people coming to know Jesus, as they were so hungry spiritually.

Healing Evangelism

Healing Evangelism works much the same way, except this power tool is the healing power of the Holy Spirit.

Carol Arnott told me a story about being in the nail salon getting her nails done, when a lady came into the shop and said she wanted her nails done similar to what Carol had. They exchanged light conversation until Carol all of a sudden said, "You have pain in your body." The lady was amazed and said, "How did you know?" As it turned out, the woman had some sort of neck injury from an accident and had been in pain ever since. Carol first helped the woman work through forgiving the person who was responsible for the accident. She then prayed with the woman and all the pain immediately left. Carol said, "That was Jesus on the outside, now would you like Him on the inside?" The woman gave her life to Jesus and promised to come to church.

Another time, John and I were on vacation and the Lord spoke to John. He told him that He would heal the first person we met that day. At breakfast an older man came up to us and started talking. He had been a soldier in World War II. When we asked him if he had pain, he said he had pain in his knee for 60 years since he was shot in the knee. The bullet went in one side and out the other. We asked if we could pray for him, which he agreed. The pain left immediately and as a result the man gave his life to Jesus.

John Wimber called it Power Evangelism. Seeing miracles and healing help bring people to salvation. There is a large percentage of the population who are in need, some in desperate need for physical healing as well as a word from the Lord.

BOLDNESS

Bill Johnson says this: "It is unnatural for a Christian to not have an appetite for the impossible. It is time the world saw some proof, some demonstration of the Kingdom of God."[47] In Ephesians 6, Paul says we are to pray always with all prayer and supplication in the Spirit. He also asks for prayer in verse 19 that *"utterance may be given to me, that I may open my mouth boldly to make known the mystery of the gospel."* We are to open our mouths boldly to make known the mystery of the gospel. Boldness is another power tool, direct from the Holy Spirit.

The early church was experiencing persecution including death and imprisonment; yet even so the apostles witnessed with boldness. Note Acts 4:13, *"Now when they saw the boldness of Peter and John, and perceived that they were uneducated and untrained men, they marveled. And they realized that they had been with Jesus."* Boldness is fostered in time abiding in the Presence of God.

That word "boldness" comes from the Greek word *parrhesia*, which means, "outspokenness, unreserved utterance, freedom of speech." Here it donates a divine enablement that comes to ordinary and unprofessional people exhibiting spiritual power and authority. It also refers to a clear presentation of the gospel without being ambiguous or unintelligible. *Parrhesia* is not a human quality but a result of being filled with the Holy Spirit.

Our job is to help bring Heaven to earth: on earth as it is in Heaven. Heaven is leading us and Heaven will back us.

THE AWAKENED HEART

The prophetically awakened heart begins with an encounter with the Living God by way of salvation. The Holy Spirit comes to inhabit us, desires to speak to us, and speak through us.

If desired, we can grow in sensitivity to the voice of God and experiences of the revelatory. Fellowshipping with the Holy Spirit, asking for revelation, and pressing in for a greater depth of revelatory knowledge are key for accessing more.

I have heard Mike Bickle preach, "To walk in the Spirit means walking in the inspiration of the Holy Spirit. You will not walk in the Spirit any more than you talk to the Spirit." It is in cultivating dynamic devotion and wholehearted, focused pursuit of Jesus that help awaken our hearts. Out of communion with the Lord, our spiritual antennae get activated and we begin to receive signals that bring understanding. The awakened heart leads to an awakened ear, which helps lead to the awakened prayer warrior, which helps lead to church and city awakening, which feeds into the global awakening we are heading into, helping to lead to the return of the Bridegroom and the Wedding to come.

From Jeremiah 23, we see some prophetic truths:

> *For who has stood in the counsel of the Lord, and has perceived and heard His word? Who has marked His word and heard it?…But if they had stood in My counsel, and had caused my people to hear My words, then they would have turned them from their evil way and from the evil of their doings…. "The prophet who has a dream, let him tell a dream; and he who has My word, let him speak My word faithfully…Is not My word like a fire?" says the Lord, "and like a hammer that breaks the rock in pieces?"* (Jeremiah 23:18,22,28-29)

There is an invitation to stand in the counsel of the Lord. From that place we can speak God's words that are like a fire in that they stir hearts, and like a hammer in that they break lies, including cultural or religious mindsets contrary to the ways of God. They can also help turn people to the Lord.

How do we grow in prophecy? First of all by cultivating an intimate relationship with the Lord. The extent of your prophetic gift depends on intimacy with the One who speaks truth. One can also pursue the gift of prophecy by asking the Lord to awaken it in your life. Position yourself regularly to hear the voice of God. Ask for dreams and visions. Honor revelation you receive by writing it out in a journal, praying into it, and obeying directives from the Lord, confirmed by seasoned others as indeed originating in God's heart. If you are having a hard time hearing God, go back to the last thing He spoke to you that you didn't do. Love, hear, and obey!

The Power of the Word

Chapter 15

JOY IN THE WORD

Your word is a lamp to my feet and a light to my path.
—Psalm 119:105

The Word of God is more fun than reading a novel, watching a movie, or viewing a beautiful sunset. It is rich in growth producing nutrients and sustenance that feeds our soul. It is life changing, an agent of transformation, and a delight.

I did not always believe that. The Bible used to seem boring to me, a duty to read, not comprehensible. One of the roles of the Holy Spirit is to teach us (see John 14:26), and thankfully I did not give up but pressed in to know and understand the Word. I'm so grateful, since my life will never be the same.

I am not a theologian, hence technicalities and doctrine you will not find here. However, I will share for the ordinary believer helpful lessons in how to become a person of the Word.

HOW DID WE GET THE BIBLE?

Approximately 40 different authors, under the inspiration of the Holy Spirit, wrote the Bible over the course of about 1500 years. The Old Testament has 39 books written in Hebrew, and the New Testament has 27 books written in Greek.

The Canon of Scripture

The term "canon" comes from the Greek *kanon* meaning "rule" or "measuring stick," as in a standard for testing straightness or accuracy. The biblical canons refer to the books regarded as divinely inspired, constituting the Bible. The term "closed canon" means books cannot be added or removed. The canonization of the Bible occurred over a process of time, and no one person or council made a book "scripture."

The closely-knit Jewish communities have regarded the Old Testament scriptures as canon for many centuries, agreed upon by conservative Christians. The scribes took great care to copy and meticulously care for the sacred texts to assure the accurate transmission of the manuscripts. The original copies of the Old Testament were written on leather or papyrus from the time of Moses (1450 B.C.) to the time of Malachi (400 B.C.). Scribes known as Masoretes had strict measures to ensure every new copy was an exact reproduction of the original.

The discovery of the Dead Sea Scrolls in 1947 gave a Hebrew text from the second to first century B.C. for all but one of the books (Esther) from the Old Testament. This discovery proved again the accuracy of the translations of the manuscripts of the Old

Testament through time.[48] The only issue of debate regarding the Old Testament scriptures was the Apocrypha, extra-biblical writings of unknown authorship. The vast majority of the Hebrew scholars considered the Apocrypha to be good historical and religious documents, but not on the same level as the Hebrew scriptures.[49]

Canonizing the New Testament

The canonization of the New Testament was considered complete by A.D. 397 with the Council of Carthage, but began much earlier with the Muratorian Canon of A.D. 170. The Council of Laodicea of A.D. 363 also stated only the Old Testament and the 27 books of the New Testament were to be read in churches as well as the Council of Hippo A.D. 393.[50]

Tests to determine if a book were to be included in canonized scripture included the following: The document needed to give evidence of being God breathed; it was to bear evidence of high moral and spiritual values that would reflect the work of the Holy Spirit; and the document had to be consistent with the orthodoxy, the Christian truth, recognized as normative in the churches.

Regarding authorship, some sort of apostolicity was required, which as a criterion, came to include those who were in immediate contact with the apostles. In other words, was the author an apostle or did he have the endorsement of an apostle? Mark wrote the gospel of Mark, but he did so under Peter's endorsement. Luke, as a close associate of the Apostle Paul, wrote under the endorsement of his authority.

Lastly, "a document's widespread and continuous acceptance and usage by churches everywhere" was taken into consideration. Put another way, universal acceptance by the church at large was another key factor in determining canonization.[51]

Ultimately, it was God who determined what books were to be included in the canonized scripture. He simply convinced His followers which books should be included in the Bible.

THE RELIABILITY OF THE BIBLE

The Bible does not need defending as those of faith will attest. Charles Spurgeon once quipped, "Defend the Bible? I'd sooner defend a lion!"[52] However, there are various means by which we can attest to the Bible's reliability. First of all, the bibliographic test looks at ancient manuscripts of the Bible and asks whether the text of the Bible we have today is the same as the original. The answer is yes. Today, there are now more than 5,300 known Greek manuscripts of the New Testament. There are 10,000 Latin Vulgate, and at least 9,300 other early versions making 24,000 manuscript copies of portions of the New Testament.[53] No other document of antiquity comes near such numbers and attestation.

The internal test asks whether we can determine if eyewitnesses wrote the document. In the New Testament we have multiple authors writing about the life of Jesus Christ, such as Matthew, Mark, Luke, John, and Paul. In other words, you have several eyewitnesses attesting to the accounts, written as historical fact.

External Evidence

External evidence for the Bible comes through tests such as archaeology or through other non-Christian historians. Regarding archaeology, Millar Burrows, a former professor of archaeology at Yale writes, "On the whole…archaeological work has unquestionably strengthened confidence in the reliability of the Scriptural record. More than one archaeologist has found his respect for the Bible increased by the experience of excavation in Palestine. Archaeology has in many cases refuted the views of modern critics."[54]

One example is John's reference in John 5:2 of *"in Jerusalem, by the Sheep Gate a pool, which is called in Hebrew, Bethesda, having five porches."* Until the 20th Century, there was no evidence outside of John's Gospel for such a place, and critics questioned John's reliability. Then in the late 1930s, the pool was uncovered by archeologists—complete with four colonnades around the edges and one across the middle.[55]

Recently, while in Israel, I visited the site of new excavations still underway. In 2009 a Catholic priest by the name of Juan Solana bought some property by the Sea of Galilee and was required to do exploratory excavation under Israeli law. The excavations uncovered the ancient town of Magdala, including the ruins of a 1st Century AD synagogue and the possible home of Mary Magdalene (Mary from Magdala).[56]

Other Historians

The writings of Jewish historian Flavius Josephus (37-100 A.D.) have proven the authenticity of scripture. Josephus was not a follower of Jesus, and yet his historical writings verify the scriptures again and again. He makes references to Jesus as well as other New Testament characters such as John the Baptist and James the brother of Jesus.[57]

Historians, archeologists and scientists prove the reliability of the scriptures as an accurate historical account. Yet more importantly, it is proven as the Word of God by the witness of the Holy Spirit in the lives of believers in Jesus.

A BIBLICAL WORLDVIEW

In short, a worldview is the overall perspective from which one sees and interprets the world. In other words, it is the set of lenses

A LIFESTYLE OF DIVINE ENCOUNTERS

through which we view life and the world. One's worldview is directly related to his or her moral beliefs and actions.

David Sliker, Director of the International House of Prayer University in Kansas City, outlines ten spheres of life through which we view truth as it pertains to the world:

- Theology: What is true about God?

- Philosophy: What is true about reality?

- Biology: What is true about life and its origins?

- Psychology: What is true about man and his nature?

- Ethics: What is true about right conduct?

- Sociology: What is true about society and people interacting with one another?

- Law: What is true about how society should be ordered?

- Politics: What is true about how society should be governed?

- Economics: What is true about how society should distribute and acquire resources?

- History: What is true in our past regarding what men have done, and why they did it?[58]

Jesus said in John 14:6, *"I am the way, the truth, and the life. No one comes to the Father except through Me."* He stated to Pilate recorded in John 18:37, *"You say rightly that I am a king. For this cause I was born, and for this cause I have come into the world, that I should bear witness to the truth. Everyone who is of the truth hears My voice."* To this Pilate retorted, *"What is truth?"* (John 18:38).

The answer to Pilate's question is of epic importance. What is truth? He was staring truth in the face and did not know it. Jesus is the epitome of truth.

Holding a biblical worldview or looking through the lenses of what God says is truth is of utmost importance as we navigate through life. We can also expect bombardment from our current culture to oppose a biblical worldview. A survey completed by the Barna Research Group determined that only 4 percent of Americans have a biblical worldview.[59]

Socrates, Plato and Aristotle set in place a worldview that still permeates much of modern society. Aristotle was the tutor of Alexander the Great, a Greek who conquered the known world in the 4th Century and set up Hellenistic centers of education and thought that propagated the philosophy of Socrates thinking.[60] Basically, the philosophy proliferated was if something was beyond reasoning, or measured scientifically, it was not relevant.[61] Therefore, the concepts of Heaven, hell, and God were relegated to less important views of the world and life.

The Age of Enlightenment of the 18th Century enhanced the concept of reason as the primary source of authority. It advanced ideals such as liberalism, progress, tolerance and separation of church and state.[62]

So much of the teaching in schools, universities, colleges, and even permeating Christian institutions is not of a biblical worldview but rather of a humanistic, rationalistic view. Going back to the truth of the scripture as the basis with which we view life is so crucial.

Chapter 16

THE WORD AND THE SPIRIT

y grandfather was a man of the Word. He had many shelves laden with books, most of which were different versions of the Bible, concordances, commentaries, and Bible reference books. My childhood memories include seeing him sitting in his favorite reclining chair reading the Bible.

I called him Opa, the Dutch name for grandfather. Although he immigrated to the United States after World War II from the Netherlands, his heritage generations earlier was French. His ancestors were Huguenots, French Protestant believers who underwent severe persecution under the rule of Louis XIV. The Edict of Fontainebleau in 1685 abolished all legal recognition of Protestantism in France. Nearly three-quarters of the Huguenots were killed and some 500,000 of them fled France by the early 18th Century. Our ancestors found refuge in Holland.[63]

My grandfather was certainly a man of the Word. However, I don't ever recall that he had a living knowledge of the Spirit of God, or the work of miracles, signs or wonders.

Spirit and Word

On the other hand, there are prophetic people who do embrace the Spirit of God but are lacking in the knowledge of the Word of God. A pastor, known in some circles to be quite prophetic, stated to me that the Lord told him the trumpet judgments spoken of in the book of Revelation had already happened as he had "heard" trumpets blowing in the Spirit. Now that is really shady theology, since at the seventh trumpet the Word of God clearly states in seven different passages that Jesus will come again. So we better hope the trumpets have not already blown or we really missed something! (See Revelation 11:15; 10:7; Isaiah 27:13; Matthew 24:31; 1 Corinthians. 15:52; 1 Thessalonians. 4:16.)

A common saying bears much truth, "If you have the Word without the Spirit you will dry up. If you have the Spirit without the Word you will blow up. But if you have the Word and the Spirit, you will grow up." We need both the Word and the Spirit.

Smith Wigglesworth, the great healing evangelist from the United Kingdom, prophesied in 1947 that in the later days there would be a "coming together of those with an emphasis on the Word and those with an emphasis on the Spirit. When the Word and the Spirit come together, there will be the biggest movement of the Holy Spirit that the nation, and indeed the world, has ever seen. It will mark the beginning of a revival that will eclipse anything that has been witnessed."[64] Amen!

LOVE FOR THE WORD

A redemptive storyline is woven all through the scriptures. It is a story of the love of a Father, who created man in His image for relationship, how that relationship was lost, the execution of His plan to restore that relationship and yet still remain just, and the future wedding to come of His Son to this Bride He had called from mankind to live and reign together forever. What a brilliant story line, of which we are called to be an integral part. Life is so much more than birth, breath, and death.

It is important to have a focused life in the Word of God to develop wisdom and sound biblical knowledge. Hebrews 4:12 states, *"The word of God is living and powerful, and sharper than any two-edged sword, piercing even to the division of soul and spirit, and of joints and marrow, and is a discerner of the thoughts and intents of the heart."* The Word of God helps decipher what is true and what is not, what matters and what doesn't, what is eternal and what is temporal.

Power to Transform

God's Word has power to transform us into His image and empower us to believe and apply His words. First Thessalonians 2:13 says, *"For this reason we also thank God without ceasing, because when you received the word of God which you heard from us, you welcomed it not as the word of men, but as it is in truth, the word of God, which also effectively works in you who believe."* The Greek word for "effectively" is *energeo*, which is one of the energy words and has to do with the active operation or working of power and its effectual results.

We can't help but be changed as we take the time to meditate on the richness of the Word of God. It works in us and transforms us. As my husband John likes to say, "We may read the Word, but really the Word reads us." The Apostle Paul stated to Timothy in Second Timothy 3:15-17:

> *Fom childhood you have known the Holy scriptures, which are able to make you wise for salvation through faith which is in Christ Jesus. All scripture is given by inspiration of God, and is profitable for doctrine, for reproof, for correction, for instruction in righteous-ness, that the man of God may be complete, thoroughly equipped for every good work.*

Overcoming Temptation

When Jesus was tempted by the devil in the wilderness, He overcame every temptation by stating, *"It is written...."* Jesus knew the authority of the Word of God as truth. Since the devil is a liar, he will continuously give mankind lies to believe about them-selves, about God, about others. The tragedy is when those lies are believed and lived out in the lives of the lost—and many believers as well. Again, Heaven and hell are both looking for human agree-ment. Who are you going to agree with?

God's Smuggler

I was a young adult on a mission's trip that involved smuggling Bibles into China from Hong Kong. We arrived at the Chinese border via hovercraft, laden with precious Bibles in our bags and within the clothes we wore. We were told, as foreigners, we would not be frisked at the border.

The Bibles in my bag were discovered and a discussion with border guards ensued. I argued for my right to carry books and the border guard asked me to read the Bible, which of course I couldn't, since they were in Cantonese. Suddenly, one border guard left the room and the second one put the Bibles back in my bag and commanded me to go. We miraculously got 500 Bibles through the border that day. We then had to act as tourists since the Bibles were delivered secretly to the underground church at night, under the cover of darkness. We were told not to pray in tongues in our hotel rooms as our rooms were under wired surveillance by authorities and we could be speaking one of the 300 different Chinese dialects.

I was deeply affected by that experience. I thought of the seven or so Bibles I had at home, most of which were collecting dust. I determined to study the Word of God after that trip.

The Blood of Martyrs

The blood of many martyrs was shed so you and I could have a Bible in our hands in our language. Wycliffe, the great Bible translator, took persecution for his stand that all should be able to read the Word and have a Bible. William Tyndale, who translated the scriptures into English and using the new medium of print, produced copies to be distributed widely. The price he paid was being strangled and burned at the stake in 1536. In 1517 seven believers in Coventry, England were burned at the stake simply for teaching their children to memorize the Lord's Prayer.

The book *Jesus Freaks* tells the story of a modern-day Chinese underground church which was raided by police. The congregants were told to spit on the Bible placed in the center of the room and if they did so, they would be allowed to leave. Starting with the pastor, one by one, they spit on the Bible and exited the room. That is until a 16-year-old wiped the spit off the Bible, repenting for how the others had denied and dishonored the Word. A gun was placed to her head. The trigger was pulled.[65]

Honor the Word

Are we honoring, studying, and hiding in our hearts this precious Word given to us? Paul admonishes Timothy in First Timothy

4:13 to give attention to reading; but in Second Timothy 2:15 he emphasizes studying like a worker: *"Be diligent to present yourself approved to God, a worker who does not need to be ashamed, rightly dividing the word of truth."* Correct application of God's Word is the result of diligent study.

If believers took stock of how much time they actually spent in reading and studying the Word of God, most would be shocked at how little time they invest in such an important tool for Christian growth and maturity. Simple yet profound is the principle of diligence in the daily.

Richard Foster begins his classic book, *Celebration of Discipline: The Path to Spiritual Growth*, stating: "Superficiality is the curse of our age. The doctrine of instant satisfaction is a primary spiritual problem. The desperate need today is not for a greater number of intelligent people, or gifted people, but for deep people."[66]

Depth of revelation of the Word of God comes through time spent reading, studying and meditating on the truths within. May we be gripped with a love for the scriptures and Holy Spirit inspired understanding.

CHILDREN AND THE WORD

Desiring to see our children love the Word means making room for teaching the Word of God to our children in a joy-filled manner. A habit John and I have exercised all our married life is to read a portion of scripture at the breakfast and dinner table as we gather together as a family. When the children started coming along, we changed our reading to come from a children's Bible accurate to the original texts, our favorite being the Golden Children's Bible. We will then ask our children questions from the passage to see how sharply everyone was listening! It has proved, over the years, to give our children a solid foundation of biblical knowledge as well as to be a fun family exercise. Additionally, John has both read the Word and helped our children memorize passages from the Bible each evening at bedtime. To this day, this practice continues with our youngest two children.

Once our children learn to read, they are instructed to have their own time with the Lord, including the reading and study of the Word. Our youngest child, Glory Anna, at the time of this writing, is 13 years old. She is diligent in her daily routine with the Lord, including time in the Bible. Our 16-year-old, Zoe, is very knowledgeable in the Bible and often will discuss the meaning of various passages she is studying with her Dad or me. Phoebe, who is 18 and has a developmental delay, has her own Bible and journal perched beside her bed, which are used at least occasionally. Aquila, age 21 and who lives in Geneva, Switzerland with her Swiss husband, graduated from the Forerunner Music Academy's Bible and worship program and is daily in the Word. Aquila's husband, Yannick Tendon, graduated from four years of theological studies at the International House of Prayer before obtaining a great job at a very influential Swiss company.

Our 23-year-old daughter Gabrielle graduated from the International House of Prayer University four-year theology program and is not only very knowledgeable in the Word but a teacher of the Word alongside Benjamin Nunez, her husband and brilliant Bible teacher. Both of them are on staff at IHOP-KC. Our oldest child and only son, Judah, is a youth leader and along with his wife, Bethany, is daily seeking the Lord in the Word. Their three young children already show a keen interest in the Bible. Hasten, three years old, recently watched his mom cut mushrooms to put in a frying pan, which was hot on the stove. He commented, "That reminds me of satan being thrown into the lake of fire."

Indeed instilling in our children a love for the Author of the Word and for the Word itself reaps abundant fruit for generations to come.

Chapter 17

STUDYING THE BIBLE

$\mathcal{G}$od has a plan for how you spend your life resources. If we seek His wisdom, we will know how to invest those resources. Life resources include time, affections, money, talents, and our energy.

Time is life. To squander time is to squander life but more importantly to squander destiny. To squander destiny is a tragic thing. But the way you squander destiny has to do with how you manage your daily life and your time.

We need to determine what our overall life vision is or, put another way, our primary purpose in life. Then we can apply our life vision to each specific area of life. Once we have that determined, our life goals need to be applied to each specific area of life including in long-term and short-term goals.

Areas of our life that we develop include:

- Spiritual (prayer time, fasting, Bible study)

- Relational (family, friends)
- Vocation (marketplace calling)
- Ministry (in the church, outside the church)
- Economicas (spending, giving, saving, investing)
- Physical (exercise, health, diet)
- Rest (recreation, vacation, play, entertainment, sports)

Schedule

Mike Bickle teaches having an action plan for our lives that reflect each long- and short-term goal in each area of our lives. And to develop a schedule for these areas which helps us to focus our priorities.[67] If you scheduled Bible study time in your daily routine, you will be much more likely to do it. Even if you don't always keep the schedule, having it there in your diary, or however you organize your life, will help you be more diligent.

Life Vision

If we have an overall life vision to love the Lord with all our heart, soul, mind and strength, (there will be other life visions that can be more specific and align with that) we will want that to be reflected in each area of our life. We love the Lord in our spirituality but also love Him as we love our spouse and family, as we live godly in our jobs, and are used of Him in ministry. We reflect our love for Him in our spending and giving, how we take care of the temple (our body) He has given us, and the choices we make for rest and entertainment.

How tragic when one area of life becomes consuming to the neglect of the rest. For example, some pursue economic prosperity in their jobs with much of their time spent working to the neglect of their marriage, children, church attendance, and spiritual development. Others may pursue spiritual development in Bible study, church attendance, meetings, conferences, mission trips, and ministry to the neglect of family, wise financial management, or physical health, and rest. Having a godly balance or schedule is very important in life.

In a study of pastors, 80 percent of pastors surveyed spend less than 15 minutes a day in prayer. Seventy percent said the only time they spend studying the Word is when they are preparing their sermons.[68] These statistics show a tragedy. One has to wonder, if this is the life of many pastors, what is the state of the body of Christ in terms of their time spent in prayer and the Word? May the Lord help us make needed adjustments.

BIBLE VERSION

The version or translation of the Bible one uses is often of personal preference. However, I will share my opinion here. Giving a new believer a King James Version of the Bible may not be helpful, since the wording and style of reading may be difficult to understand. As a younger person, I used the New International Version translation. I know others who like The Message or other similar easy-to-read versions.

My personal preference now and for study purposes is the New King James Version. If you are shopping for a new Bible, I recommend the New Spirit-Filled Life Bible, New King James Version, which has commentaries from Spirit-filled leaders edited by Jack Hayford. It has great study notes, a concordance, and a "Word Wealth" section explaining the Hebrew or Greek meaning of many key words.

E-book vs. Paper Book

Reading the Word on a computer, tablet, or phone may be convenient when in a meeting or when out and about. However, I highly recommend using a written Bible as your main source of study and reading. There is something about the written pages that help one memorize, understand, be able to highlight, write in the margins, and reread that is very helpful. A woman came to me to testify that she had heard me say a paper Bible is best to use as your primary Bible source. She had decided to then abandon only reading on a tablet and bought a Bible. The change to her time in the Word was dramatic, much deeper and more meaningful to her.

READ THROUGH

When a survey was taken in a church of how many believers had read through the entire Bible, only 10 percent of those in attendance raised their hands to the affirmative. That seems tragic if such a low percentage of believers have read the whole of the Word.

The whole counsel of the Word of God is rich for our growth. Don't just skip here and there or play frequent "Bible roulette" (randomly opening the Bible to read a passage). Read through the 66 books of the Bible.

I recommend reading through a portion of the Old Testament and New Testament every day. Start reading in Genesis and in Matthew and read through. When finishing in Malachi, start over in Genesis; and when you finish Revelation, start over in Matthew. I also add reading a Proverb a day, one for each day of the month.

If we leave out reading and studying the Old Testament, we are at a greater handicap of understanding the plan of redemption the Father has woven all through history to bring us into relationship with Him.

MEDITATION

Joshua 1:8 states, *"This Book of the Law shall not depart from your mouth, but you shall meditate in it day and night, that you may observe to do according to all that is written in it. For then you will make your way prosperous, and then you will have good success."* What is the recipe for prosperity and good success? Meditation on the Word of God!

The word "meditate" in Hebrew is *hagah,* meaning "to mutter or ponder out loud to oneself." Unlike an English definition of meditate, which is more of a mental exercise, the Hebrew thought of meditation of the scriptures involves quiet repeating of the Word while bypassing distractions. Jewish prayer called "davening" involves reciting texts, praying prayers or communing with God while bowing or rocking back and forth. I have heard that this motion actually helps the brain retain and learn more.

This form of meditation can include praying the Bible as well as prophetic decrees, discussed in the section of the book on prayer.

PRAYING PORTIONS OF THE WORD

The written Word is to be a door through which we gain entry into the Living Word—Jesus Himself.

Jesus was speaking to the religious leaders when He said in John 5:39-40, *"You search the scriptures, for in them you think you have eternal life; and these are they which testify of Me. But you are not willing to come to Me that you may have life."* The words and letters of the scriptures themselves do not contain life, but it is the written Word leading us to the Living Word—Jesus Himself—that does produce life. We can come to Him, and access Him through Spirit-inspired meditation of His Word.

As covered earlier in this book, turn passages of the Word of God into prayer. If a particular verse admonishes us to obey, make it into declarations such as, "I set my heart to obey you in this directive. Strengthen me to heed your words and build my life on the rock of your commands." (see Matt. 7:24-29) If a passage expresses a truth we are to believe, we can thank God for this truth and ask Him to reveal more of His heart to us as it pertains to that truth. Turn the Word into meditative dialogue with the Author.

Write Out Revelation

Have your journal handy and write out revelation you receive from your study of the Word. It is a principle of learning that one will be much more likely to remember and understand something if you record what you learn.

Sing the Bible

Singing the Word of God is a powerful way to learn passages, receive it into your heart, and put a creative, prophetic spin to the Word. We have sets in our House of Prayer, known as "Worship in the Word," where we sing the Word. They are enveloped in the Presence of God. The book of Psalms is filled with songs meant to be sung, although singing the Word is not limited to the Psalms.

STUDYING A BOOK OF THE BIBLE

The Word of God has many depths of meaning and revelation. Of the many years I have read and studied the Bible, every day I receive new or deeper revelation.

Taking a book of the Bible to study more in-depth can prove very helpful in gaining greater understanding of the expanse of meaning in the Word. Studying a book can look like reading a particular passage or chapter while simultaneously reading corresponding commentaries for that book and passage, inquiring of the Lord for more understanding, and looking into historical and geographical context.

The best commentary I know of for the Book of Revelation is *Study Guide for the Book of Revelation* by Mike Bickle. There are also commentaries available online such as www.soniclight.com. To access commentaries, you click on "Study Notes," and the expository Bible study notes written by Dr. Thomas Constable for each of the books of the Bible are free to access.

Other helpful aspects of Bible study are to know the culture of the times from which the passages were written. For example, Paul's admonishing women in First Corinthians 14:34-35 has been skewed in interpretation by numerous factions of the body of Christ for many years: *"Let your women keep silent in the churches, for they are not permitted to speak; but they are to be submissive, as the law also says. And if they want to learn something, let them ask their own husbands at home: for it is shameful for women to speak in church."* At that time, men and women sat on differing sides of the church. Women, in boldness, would be disruptive as they spoke loudly to their husbands on the other side of the building asking questions. Hence Paul said, *"Let them ask their own husbands at home."* This was not to be taken to mean women could never speak or prophesy or preach in a church context.

Knowing the land of the Bible is helpful to understand the stories therein. That is why most Bibles have maps included from biblical times. We own a satellite map of the Holy Land, which helps understand certain passages and the topography within. Additionally, John and I lead yearly teaching tours of Israel with an excellent messianic guide by the name of Arie Bar David. We have learned tremendously from these trips, being on the land, opening our Bibles to study at the very place where the stories took place centuries earlier.

Other online resources I recommend for bible study include the free online concordance of www.biblegateway.com. Years ago I actually used to carry around a huge, thick Strong's Concordance, wanting to get the right meaning of words. It is much easier now to have online resources.

I know of some who have signed up with Christian Broadcasting Network to receive daily emails specifying the Bible passage to read that day in order to read through the Bible in one year (www.cbn.com). CBN's news is also an excellent resource to learn about what God is up to in the world instead of the primarily negative news reported on the major news networks.

Another online website with helpful devotionals and resources is called Crosswalk (http://www.crosswalk.com).

A top-of-the-line Bible study computer software can be found in a program called Accordance (http://www.accordancebible.com). It has all the resources together—concordance, Greek and Hebrew word meanings, maps, study guides, commentaries, and more.

The online resource I use the most is Mike Bickle's online teaching library (www.mikebickle.org). New weekly teachings are added as well as an abundance of teachings on various topics and books of the Bible.

PSALM 119

Psalm 119 is full of wisdom about the Word of God. Below are some pertinent verses to meditate on concerning the Word from this rich chapter, which happens to be the longest in the Bible.

How can a young man cleanse his way? By taking heed according to Your word. With my whole heart I have sought You; oh, let me not wander from Your commandments! Your word I have hidden in my heart, that I might not sin against You (Verse 9-11).

I will meditate on Your precepts, and contemplate Your ways. (Verse 15).

Open my eyes, that I may see wondrous things from your law (Verse 18).

I will run the course of Your commandments, for You shall enlarge my heart (Verse 32).

Turn away my eyes from looking at worthless things, and revive me in Your way (Verse 37).

The law of Your mouth is better to me than thousands of coins of gold and silver (Verse 72).

Forever, O Lord, Your word is settled in Heaven. Your faithfulness endures to all generations (Verses 89-90).

Your word is a lamp to my feet and a light to my path (Verse 105).

The entrance of Your words gives light; it gives understanding to the simple. I opened my mouth and panted, for I longed for Your commandments (Verses 130-131).

I rise before the dawning of the morning, and cry for help; I hope in Your word. My eyes are awake through the night watches, that I may meditate on Your word (Verses 147-148).

The entirety of Your word is truth, and every one of Your righteous judgments endures forever (Verse 160).

Great peace have those who love Your law, and nothing causes them to stumble (Verse 165).

THE STUDY OF END TIMES

The year was 2008 and the words of God were spoken clearly into my spirit, "Patricia, how is it that I've made you a prophetic voice but you have no idea about the particulars of the greatest prophesy of all time—My coming again." I could only respond, "Good point, God."

So I began to search out and study the more than 150 chapters in the Bible that speak of end times. I began to be fascinated by not just the detail the scripture gives of the times surrounding the second coming of Jesus; but even more so, I was fascinated to a new degree by this man, Jesus Christ, who is truly coming back as a King, a Judge, and even more personally, as a Bridegroom to me and all who love Him.

The first five words of the book of Revelation are, "The revelation of Jesus Christ." I love Him. I want to know this revelation about Him.

I discovered that it was my right or privilege as a child of the day to know about His coming.

> *But concerning the times and the seasons, brethren, you have no need that I should write to you. For you yourselves know perfectly that the day of the Lord so comes as a thief in the night. For when they say 'Peace and safety!' then sudden destruction comes upon them, as labor pains upon a pregnant woman. And they shall not escape. But you, brethren are not in darkness, so that this Day should overtake you as a thief. You are all sons of the light and sons of the day. We are not of the night or of the darkness.*

Therefore, let us not sleep, as others do, but let us watch and be sober. For those who sleep, sleep at night, and those who get drunk are drunk at night. But let us who are of the day be sober, putting on the breastplate of faith and love, and as a helmet the hope of salvation. For God did not appoint us to wrath, but to obtain salvation through our Lord Jesus Christ (1 Thessalonians 5:1-9).

Controversy?

There has been a lie propagated that the study of the end times is too controversial as well as impossible to understand. However, as we give ourselves to diligent study of the Word as it pertains to the time of the end, we discover many clear passages that parallel each other. When we gain biblical understanding, we come into greater unity as the body of Christ. Speaking in the context of end times, Jeremiah 23:20 says, *"In the latter days you will understand it perfectly."*

Rewards to those who press into understanding the scriptures as it pertains to the end times includes being wise, able to instruct many, and shining before the Lord. Daniel 12:3 says, *"Those who are wise shall shine like the brightness of the firmament, and those who turn many to righteousness like the stars forever and ever."* Daniel 11:32-33 says, *"The people who know their God shall be strong, and carry out great exploits. And those of the people who understand shall instruct many."*

CONCLUSION

The Word of God is precious, life giving, and anointed. Prayer is wonderful communion with the personal God who loves to hear our voice raised to Him. Living a prophetic life is vital in enhancing our ability to receive and live out of revelation from a loving Father.

Taking time in our lives to pray, hear the voice of God, and meditate on the Word will yield great fruit as we grow in the knowledge of God and His eternal plan. We find our identity as children of a loving Father, who breathed the words of life we read and hear. Our call to be a Bride, wholly given to Bridegroom Jesus, becomes clear. We live empowered lives under the leadership of the Holy Spirit.

Let us step into the story line of the ages knowing we have a role to play in the great end-time drama that will unfold. Heavenly great clouds of witnesses are cheering us on. Jesus is interceding for us and beckoning us (see Rom. 8:34). We live in a most spectacular time in history. Let's live it for what really counts. Let's live life abandoned to the One who is worthy of all.

ENDNOTES

1. Jeanne Guyon, *Experiencing the Depths of Jesus Christ* (Jacksonville, FL: SeedSowers Christian Books Publishing House, 1975), 25.

2. Bill Johnson, *Release the Power of Jesus* (Shippensburg, PA: Destiny Image Publishers, 2009).

3. Henri J.M. Nouwen, *In the Name of Jesus* (New York, NY: The Crossroad Publishing Company, 1989), 55.

4. Mike Bickle, *Growing in Prayer* (Lake Mary, FL: Charisma House, 2014), 33.

5. Elijah List, "History Belongs to the Intercessor," 2005, http://www.elijahlist.com/words/display_word/3550.

6. Dick Eastman, *No Easy Road* (Ada, MI: Chosen Books, 2003), 94.

7. Hope Faith Prayer, "Daniel Nash 1775-1831—Prayer Warrior for Charles Finney," 2016, https://hopefaithprayer.com/prayer-warrior-charles-finney.

8. Voice in the City, "Suzette Hattingh," https://www.voiceinthecity.org/en/about/suzette-hattingh.

9. Dr. John Caldwell, *Intimacy with God* (LaVerge, TN: Xulon Press, 2009), 40.

10. Evan Wiggs, "These Prayed: General William Booth," http://www.evanwiggs.com/revival/portrait/booth.html.

11. Eastman, *No Easy Road*, 35.

12. Becky Tirabassi, *Sacred Obsession Devotional* (Carol Stream, IL: Tyndale House Publishers, 2007), 135.

13. Brother Lawrence, *The Practice of the Presence of God* (Christian Classics Ethereal Library, 1895), 32.

14. Guyon, *Depths of Jesus Christ*, 45.

15. Mark Virkler, "Health Benefits of Speaking in Tongues," *Communion with God Ministries*, 2014. http://www.cwgministries.org/blogs/health-benefits-speaking-tongues.

16. Benedict Carey, "A Neuroscientific Look at Speaking in Tongues," *The New York Times*, 2006. http://www.nytimes.com/2006/11/07/health/07brain.html?_r=0.

17. Franklin Graham, *Rebel with a Cause* (Nashville, TN: Thomas Nelson Inc., 1995).

18. Norman Grubb, *Rees Howells Intercessor* (Fort Washington, PA: CLC Publications, 1952), 64.

19. Inspirational Christians, "Rees Howells Biography," http://www.inspirationalchristians.org/biography/rees-howells.

20. Grubb, *Rees Howells Intercessor*, 87.

21. Arthur Wallis, *God's Chosen Fast* (Fort Washington, PA: CLC Publications, 1968), 89.

22. "Fasting 101: Practical Tips and Helpful Guidelines," *Luke 18 Project.com*, http://luke18project.com/blog/707/fasting-101-practical-tips-and-helpful-guidelines.

23. Ed Silvoso, *That None Should Perish* (Ada, MI: Chosen Books, 2011), 58-96.

24. C.S. Lewis, *The Screwtape Letters* (San Francisco, CA: Harper One, 1942), 39.

25. Eastman, *No Easy Road*, 62.

26. "Luther: I have so much to do that I shall have to spent the first three hours in prayer," *Beggars All Reformation and Apologetics,* July 13, 2009, http://beggarsallreformation.blogspot.ca/2009/07/luther-i-have-so-much-to-do-that-i.html.

27. E.M. Bounds, *Power Through Prayer,* June 1, 2005, https://www.ccel.org/ccel/bounds/power.I_1.html.

28. Mark Guy Pearse, "The Story of a Prayer Meeting and What Came of It," *Bible Hub.* http://biblehub.com/sermons/auth/pearse/the_story_of_a_prayer_meeting_and_what_came_of_it.htm.

29. The Hidden Ones, "Bangor, Ireland Watch, AD 55," http://hiddenonesmi.com/2012/07/31/bangor-ireland-watch-ad-555/.

30. "Bernard of Clairvaux," *Wikipedia.com,* last modified November 26, 2017, https://en.wikipedia.org/wiki/Bernard_of_Clairvaux.

31. "Nicolaus Zinzendorf," *Wikipedia.com,* last modified November 22, 2017, https://en.wikipedia.org/wiki/Nicolaus_Zinzendorf.

32. KJOS Ministries, "The Moravians and Count Zinzendorf," http://www.crossroad.to/Heaven/Excerpts/books/history/hand-of-God/moravian.htm.

33. "David Yonggi Cho," *Wikipedia.com,* last modified November 26, 2017. https://en.wikipedia.org/wiki/David_Yonggi_Cho.

34. "31 Prayer Quotes: Be Inspired and Encouraged!" *Crosswalk.com,* October, 2016, https://www.crosswalk.com/faith/spiritual-life/inspiring-quotes/31-prayer-quotes-be-inspired-and-encouraged.html.

35. Bill Johnson Ministries, http://bjm.org/qa/how-do-i-receive-revelation.

36. Bill Johnson Ministries, http://bjm.org/qa/how-do-i-receive
-revelation.

37. "Did Abraham Lincoln Predict His Own Death?" *History.com,*
October 31, 2012, http://www.history.com/news/ask-history/
did-abraham-lincoln-predict-his-own-death.

38. "Lincoln Dreams About a Presidential Assassination,"
History.com, http://www.history.com/this-day-in-history/
lincoln-dreams-about-a-presidential-assassination.

39. Eva Hart, *Eva Hart Speaks About Her Memories of the Titanic:
Survivor Interview,* video, 13:05, Novmeber 29, 2010, https://
www.youtube.com/watch?v=MD5J43Z9AWI.

40. "Titanic Passengers' Eerie Premonitions,"
PremierExhibitions.com. http://www.premierexhibitions.
com/exhibitions/3/3/titanic-artifact-exhibition/blog/titanic
-passengers-eerie-premonitions.

41. Rebecca Turner, "10 Dreams That Changed Human
History," *World of Lucid Dreaming,* http://www.
world-of-lucid-dreaming.com/10-dreams-that-changed-the-
course-of-human-history.html.

42. "Ontario Highway 401," *Wikipedia.com,* last modified
November 23, 2017, https://en.wikipedia.org/wiki/
Ontario_Highway_401.

43. Nancy Ravenhill, *Touched by Heaven* (Ada, MI: Chosen
Books, 2015), 194.

44. Randy Clark, *There is More* (Ada, MI: Chosen Books, 2013),
120.

45. Heidi Baker, *Birthing the Miraculous* (Lake Mary, FL:
Charisma House, 2014).

46. Gary B. McGee, "The Revival Legacy of Smith
Wigglesworth," *Enrichment Journal,* http://enrichmentjournal
.ag.org/199801/070_wigglesworth.cfm.

47. Bill Johnson, *The Supernatural Power of a Transformed Mind Expanded Edition: Access to a Life of Miracles* (Shippensburg: Destiny Image, Inc., 2014).

48. J. Hampton Keathley, III, "The Bible: The Holy Canon of Scripture," *Bible.org*, https://bible.org/seriespage/7-bible-holy-canon-scripture.

49. "How and When Was the Bible Put Together?" *Got Questions*, http://www.gotquestions.org/canon-Bible.html.

50. Keathley, "The Bible," *Bible.org*. https://bible.org/seriespage/7-bible-holy-canon-scripture.

51. Robert Velarde, "How Did We Get the Bible?" *Focus on the Family*, 2009, http://www.focusonthefamily.com/faith/the-study-of-god/how-do-we-know-the-bible-is-true/how-did-we-get-the-bible.

52. Andy Bannister, "Why Trust the Bible?" *Zacharias Trust*, http://www.rzim.eu/why-trust-the-bible.

53. Keathley, "The Bible," *Bible.org*, https://bible.org/seriespage/7-bible-holy-canon-scripture.

54. Bannister, "Why Trust," http://www.rzim.eu/why-trust-the-bible.

55. Ibid.

56. Mark Miller, "Archaeologists Excavate Possible Home of Mary Magdalene and Synagogue Where Jesus May Have Preached," *Ancient Origins*, August 6, 2015, http://www.ancient-origins.net/history-archaeology/archaeologists-excavate-possible-home-mary-magdalene-and-synagogue-020472.

57. "Josephus on Jesus," *Wikipedia.com*, last modified November 18, 2017, https://en.wikipedia.org/wiki/Josephus_on_Jesus.

58. David Sliker: *Introduction to Apologetics* Course Notes, Session Two.

59. Del Tackett, "What's Christian Worldview?" *Focus on the Family*, 2006. http://www.focusonthefamily.com/faith/ christian-worldview/whats-a-christian-worldview/whats -a-worldview-anyway.

60. "Alexander the Great," *Wikipedia.com*, last modified December 2, 2017. https://en.wikipedia.org/wiki/Alexander_the_Great.

61. "Socrates," *Wikipedia.com*, last modified December 5, 2017. https://en.wikipedia.org/wiki/Socrates.

62. "Age of Enlightenment," *Wikipedia.com*, last modified December 6, 2017. https://en.wikipedia.org/wiki/ Age_of_Enlightenment.

63. "Huguenots," *Wikipedia.com*, last modified December 1, 2017. https://en.wikipedia.org/wiki/Huguenot.

64. "Smith Wigglesworth's 1947 Prophetic Word," *Pray for Scotland*. http://www.prayforscotland.org.uk/smith -wigglesworths-1947-prophetic-word.

65. D.C. Talk, *Jesus Freaks* (New York, NY: Albury Publishing 1999), 137.

66. Richard Foster, *Celebration of Discipline* (New York, NY: Harper-Collins 1988), 10.

67. Mike Bickle, Creator, *The Power of a Focused: Weekly Schedule*, pdf, 2014, http://mikebickle.org/resources/resource/3587.

68. Richard Murphy, Maranatha Life, pdf, 2002, http:// markbeaird.org/wmlib/pdfarticlesstatistics_about_pastors.pdf.

ABOUT
PATRICIA BOOTSMA

*P*atricia Bootsma and her husband John, are the Senior Associate Pastors of Catch the Fire Toronto. Patricia is also the Director of the Catch the Fire House of Prayer. She leads the Ontario Prophetic Counsel and represents Ontario to the Canadian Prophetic Counsel. Patricia ministers as a prophetic voice internationally helping to inspire hearts to walk in passionate desire for the Bridegroom and live out fullness of destiny. Patricia helps start Houses of Prayer, inspiring prayer and worship in the spirit of the Tabernacle of David. John and Patricia are the parents of six wonderful children, three of whom are married with three grandchildren.

OTHER BOOKS BY PATRICIA BOOTSMA

*Raising Burning Hearts: Parenting and Mentoring
Next Generation Lovers of God*

Convergence: Heaven's Destiny Becoming Your Reality

Canada Book of Decrees and Prophecies (contributor)

FREE E-BOOKS?
YES, PLEASE!

Get **FREE** and deeply discounted **Christian books** for your **e-reader** delivered to your inbox **every week!**

IT'S SIMPLE!

VISIT lovetoreadclub.com

SUBSCRIBE by entering your email address

RECEIVE free and discounted e-book offers and inspiring articles delivered to your inbox every week!

Unsubscribe at any time.

SUBSCRIBE NOW!

LOVE TO READ CLUB

visit **LOVETOREADCLUB.COM** ▶